W9-BZA-230

KATHLEEN STANLEY, CDE, RD, MSED

AND CONNIE C. CRAWLEY, MS, RD, LD

Quick & Easy Diabetic Recipes for One

Tips and Recipes for Healthy Eating on Your Own

American Diabetes Association

BOOK ACQUISITIONS
Susan Reynolds

EDITOR
Laurie Guffey

PRODUCTION DIRECTOR
Carolyn R. Segree

PRODUCTION COORDINATOR
Peggy M. Rote

COVER & INTERIOR DESIGN
Wickham & Associates, Inc.

TYPESETTING SERVICES
Harlowe Typography, Inc.

ILLUSTRATIONS
Richard Thompson

©1997 by the American Diabetes Association, Inc. All Rights Reserved. No part of this publication may be reproduced or transmitted in any form or by any means, electronic or mechanical, including duplication, recording, or any information storage and retrieval system, without the prior written permission of the American Diabetes Association.
Printed in the United States of America

4 6 8 10 9 7 5 3

The suggestions and information contained in this publication are generally consistent with the Clinical Practice Recommendations and other policies of the American Diabetes Association, but they do not represent the policy or position of the Association or any of its boards or committees. Reasonable steps have been taken to ensure the accuracy of the information presented. However, the American Diabetes Association cannot ensure the safety or efficacy of any product or service described in this publication. Individuals are advised to consult a physician or other appropriate health care professional before undertaking any diet or exercise program or taking any medication referred to in this publication. Professionals must use and apply their own professional judgment, experience, and training and should not rely solely on the information contained in this publication before prescribing any diet, exercise, or medication. The American Diabetes Association—its officers, directors, employees, volunteers, and members—assumes no responsibility or liability for personal or other injury, loss, or damage that may result from the suggestions or information in this publication.

American Diabetes Association
1701 N. Beauregard Street
Alexandria, VA 22311

Library of Congress Cataloging-in-Publication Data
Stanley, Kathleen, 1963–
    Quick & easy diabetic recipes for one : tips and recipes for
healthy eating on your own / Kathleen Stanley and Connie C. Crawley.
        p.   cm.
    Includes index.
    ISBN 0-945448-84-8 (pbk.)
    1.   Diabetes—Diet therapy—Recipes.   2.   Cookery for one.
I.   Crawley, Connie C.,   1953– .   II.   Title.
RC662.S76   1997
616.4′620654—dc21
                                                    97-39891
                                                    CIP

Dedication

To my mom, who humored me during my early years in the kitchen, and to my husband, who adds the most important ingredient in my life.

— Kathleen Stanley

To my husband, who loves to taste-test my recipes when he gets the chance.

— Connie Crawley

Editorial Advisory Board

EDITOR-IN-CHIEF

David B. Kelley, MD
Olympia, Washington

ASSOCIATE EDITORS

Robert M. Anderson, EdD
Michigan Diabetes Research
and Training Center
The University of Michigan
Medical School
Ann Arbor, Michigan

Janine C. Freeman, RD, CDE
Georgia Center for Diabetes
at Columbia Dunwoody
Medical Center
Atlanta, Georgia

Patti Bazel Geil, MS, RD, CDE
The University of Kentucky
Hospital
Lexington, Kentucky

Marvin E. Levin, MD
Chesterfield, Missouri

Barbara J. Maschak-Carey,
RNCS, MSN, CDE
Hospital of the University of
Pennsylvania
Philadelphia, Pennsylvania

David S. Schade, MD
The University of New Mexico
School of Medicine
Albuquerque, New Mexico

MEMBERS

Samuel L. Abbate, MD, CDE
Medcenter One Health
Systems
Bismarck, North Dakota

Eva Brzezinski, RD, MS
The University of California at
San Diego Medical Center
San Diego, California

Connie C. Crawley, RD, BS, MS
The University of Georgia
Cooperative Extension
Service
Athens, Georgia

John T. Devlin, MD
Maine Medical Center
Portland, Maine

Alan M. Jacobson, MD
Joslin Diabetes Center
Boston, Massachusetts

Lois Jovanovic, MD
Sansum Medical Research
Foundation
Santa Barbara, California

Carolyn Leontos, MS, RD, CDE
The University of Nevada
Cooperative Extension
Las Vegas, Nevada

Peter A. Lodewick, MD
Diabetes Care Center
Birmingham, Alabama

Carol E. Malcom, BSN, CDE
Seattle, Washington

Wylie McNabb, EdD
The University of Chicago
Center for Medical
Education and Health Care
Chicago, Illinois

Virginia Peragallo-Dittko, RN,
MA, CDE
Winthrop University Hospital
Mineola, New York

Jacqueline Siegel, RN
St. Joseph Hospital
Seattle, Washington

Tim Wysocki, PhD
Nemours Children's Clinic
Jacksonville, Florida

Contents

Acknowledgments

THANKS TO Madelyn Wheeler, MS, RD, CDE, and Marilynn S. Arnold, MS, RD, CDE, who provided thoughtful and helpful reviews of the introductory material. Lyn Wheeler also did her usual careful job on the nutrient analysis. A few of these recipes were originally developed for the University of Georgia Cooperative Extension Service.

Introduction

YOU ALREADY KNOW how important a healthy, flexible meal plan is in controlling your diabetes. But if you're on your own, you may feel too busy, rushed, or scattered to eat well. Or you may be feeling lonely, tired, or discouraged about the effort it would take to cook something for yourself. Help is here! This book shows you how to prepare quick, nutritious meals just for you—because you deserve them, just like you deserve to always feel your best.

What, when, and how much you eat has a huge impact on your blood glucose level. Blood glucose, in turn, affects everything about how well you feel—and how much, or little, diabetes will impact your life. It's easier than you think to make just a few changes that will reap long-term benefits.

You're continually faced with food choices and food temptations during your waking hours. Food is the center of many social events, including get-togethers with friends, special family gatherings, and religious meetings. You're bombarded each day with food advertisements and dozens of local fast-food restaurants. You may have used food as a reward or for comfort in the past, or developed some habits you'd prefer to change.

The good news is that there are many different ways to eat well—and many different things you can eat! The first step is to see a registered dietitian (RD) to design your own individualized plan. This will take into account your food likes and dislikes, your exercise habits, and your daily schedule. We've learned you can be much more flexible in your food choices than we originally thought—so learn how to include that tasty dessert or previously forbidden food into your new, healthy meal plan.

HOW TO GET STARTED

Choosing the right foods and putting them together into meals can be confusing. How do you start to put together a healthy diet to last a lifetime? Daily activities and routines change, and this may affect your interest in food shopping and food preparation in many different ways. When you are a college student, you may have few choices for meals, and as a single adult, you may have little time for even basic meal preparation. As you get older, your appetite and interest in food can increase or decrease. A meal plan should be adjusted during the different stages of life, but have some basic components that allow it to be flexible enough to last a lifetime. Here are some basic tips that you may find helpful when setting up your meal plan.

- **Moderation is the key.** Learn about portion control. When you first start to cook for yourself, stick to the recommended serving sizes or amounts, even if they seem too small or large. You may have to adjust your perspective when it comes to food quantities.

- **Balance and variety are essential.** Eating the same foods over and over again may lead to boredom and frustration! If you are on a limited or restricted meal plan you just can't stick to, investigate why. Perhaps you have fallen into a habit of shopping for the same things—take a friend with you to the store and listen to his or her suggestions, or ask your dietitian for new ideas.

- **Practice in the kitchen.** Great-tasting recipes will keep you satisfied and interested in your meal plan. Practice with the recipes in this book and learn what works for you! Seek out new recipes, and learn about possible ingredient substitutions. You may be able to turn a previously "forbidden" recipe into a new healthy option. To permanently change your eating habits, begin trying one new recipe a week—in one year, you can have a whole new set of eating choices.

- **Include your favorite foods.** Your meal plan can allow satisfying portions of your favorite foods. If it doesn't, consult your dietitian or diabetes health care team to learn why. Knowledge is power: by learning about new cooking techniques and food combinations, you can find creative ways to keep your taste buds happy—and the rest of you healthy!

TIMING IS EVERYTHING

Some people will tell you that choosing foods is the hardest part of a meal plan. However, in today's busy world, sticking to a meal schedule may be just as difficult. People with diabetes need to follow a regular meal schedule so that a pattern of metabolism is established. In other words, whenever you eat something, it is digested in the body. This digestive process (the basis of metabolism) breaks down the components of food (protein, fat, and carbohydrate) into fuel (glucose).

Your body uses insulin to capture the glucose from the bloodstream and carry it into your cells and organs. A certain amount of glucose in your bloodstream is maintained at all times, but the level rises after you eat. It's best if your body knows the pattern of blood glucose rises so it can respond appropriately, or you can help it react better by adjusting your medication or exercise level.

You can't always eat at exactly the same time each day; however, being consistent will help you and your diabetes health care team manage your blood glucose levels. This may mean discussing your schedule needs with your boss, co-workers, teachers, friends, and family. When you are by yourself, it can be difficult to find the motivation to stay on a schedule. Try it, and you may find that feeling better is motivation enough!

Be prepared for unplanned events. Schedules can be upset by factors out of your control—you have to stay late at work, you have to take a business trip, you are stuck in traffic, your family requires your presence, an appointment runs late. Keep emergency snacks available for these times, and know how to adjust your next meal to account for the change.

MEAL PLANNING FOR ONE

Meal planning can make a big difference in your time and money management as well as in your blood glucose control. At first, planning a day's or week's worth of menus will seem time-consuming, but with practice you will get faster. Most people eat the same 15 to 20 foods over and over again. Within a few weeks, based on your blood glucose readings and your own personal preferences, you will know which menus work best for you.

The key to meal planning is consistency. Most people control their diabetes better if they eat about the same amount of food at regular times. The carbohydrate in your food affects your blood glucose level the most. Eating approximately the same amount of carbohydrate at the same time each day will make your blood glucose readings more predictable. Of course, other factors like illness or activity can also change your blood glucose levels, but consistent eating patterns really make a difference.

That doesn't mean you shouldn't also consider your fat and protein intake. Certainly fat and protein provide calories, and if you eat too much your blood glucose may be higher three to four hours after the meal, but they have less overall effect than carbohydrate-rich foods. High intake of fat may increase your risk for heart disease, and high intake of protein may speed up kidney complications. Obviously, balance of these nutrients is essential.

Breakfast: *Start Your Day Right*

Choose high-fiber, low-fat foods for breakfast. Good choices are cereals with at least three grams of fiber and four grams or less of sugar. Although sugar does not raise your blood glucose level any more than equal amounts of other carbohydrates, cereals high in sugar are usually not as nutritious. Choose breads like English muffins or bagels that have whole wheat listed as one of the first two ingredients. Even reduced-fat pancakes or waffles topped with cooked fruit or reduced-sugar syrup and diet margarine are a nice change.

This is also a good time to eat more fruit. Control your intake of carbohydrate better by eating whole pieces of fruit rather than drinking juice. The fiber in the fruit will make you feel more satisfied. Many people drink much more juice than they realize, and their blood glucose levels can shoot up very quickly.

Whether you have a high-protein food at this meal is up to you. You may want to eat fewer whole eggs and less high-fat cheese, and use egg whites and nonfat or low-fat cheeses. Include some nonfat milk or yogurt.

Lunch: Slow Down and Enjoy

If you are at home, lunch can be anything you want to fix, but many of us eat away from home at lunchtime. While eating out is easy, it often means eating more fat, calories, and sodium than you need. You may want to pack a lunch with leftovers from supper the night before. Or try some of the low-fat lunch meats, canned soups, and frozen entrees on the market. Homemade turkey or chicken, either sliced or diced and made into a salad with celery, pickle, and reduced-fat mayonnaise mixed half and half with plain yogurt, is a great sandwich filler. Make sandwiches on whole-wheat bread or rolls, and try reduced-fat salad dressings instead of high-fat sandwich spreads.

Salads are always great, especially if you choose plenty of fresh, low-calorie vegetables and use a minimum of reduced-fat or nonfat dressing. Top a main-dish salad with small amounts of lean poultry, beef, or shredded low-fat cheese. Good accompaniments are whole-wheat versions of pita bread, English muffins, crackers, or bagels.

If you have access to a microwave or stove, you can prepare cooked vegetables. Just season with low-sodium powdered bouillon, a commercial herb mixture, and onion. Cook for three to four minutes according to package directions. For dessert, try fruit—a different one every day! If you like sweeter desserts, there are plenty of reduced-fat desserts on the market. Substitute the carbohydrate in these desserts for other carbohydrates in your meal.

Supper: End the Day Gracefully

Many people eat very little all day and then overeat all night. This isn't healthy for anyone—you just feel lethargic and ruin your appetite for breakfast. Your evening meal can be about the same size as your lunch meal. Of course, you may choose to have your larger meal at noon. This is fine as long as you do it consistently.

Prepare meat, fish, or poultry by baking, broiling, grilling, boiling, or stir-frying. Deep-fat or panfry as little as possible. Choose side dishes that are lower in fat and higher in fiber. Good starch choices are baked white or sweet potatoes, corn, brown rice, and whole-wheat pasta. Eat them plain or seasoned with small amounts of olive oil, tomato sauce, nonfat sour cream, or soft margarine. Enjoy at least two low-calorie vegetables like broccoli, cauliflower, carrots, and green beans per meal. Whole-grain bread or rolls are so flavorful that they need very little margarine or fruit spread as a topping. Finish off your meal with some fresh fruit or a low-fat dessert.

Snacking: Keeping Your Energy Up

Most traditional snacks are high in fat, sugar, and sodium. But plenty of delicious snacks are available that will make you feel better! Try graham crackers; low-fat crackers; cereal; fruit; and nonfat or low-fat milk, cheese, and yogurt. Less common snacks are baked potatoes topped with nonfat sour cream, cut-up vegetables served with a low-fat dip, or a cup of vegetable soup. Vary your snack choices so you are less tempted to indulge at the vending machine. Carry at least one healthy snack all the time so you won't be at the mercy of a high-fat, high-sugar temptation.

Emergencies: Be Prepared

Sudden illness, bad weather, and unexpected transportation problems can potentially restrict your ability to shop for food items. If you live alone, there may not be anyone available to help with shopping during these times. It's essential that you create an "Emergency Food Shelf" and keep it stocked with nonperishable items. The shelf will prevent you from having to go hungry or having your blood glucose level drop too low. Below is a list of items you might consider buying for your shelf.

- bottled drinking water
- canned tuna, salmon, or chicken
- evaporated skim milk or nonfat dry milk powder
- instant oatmeal
- instant soup mix
- low-fat granola or breakfast bars
- non-diet soda
- peanut butter
- saltine-type crackers
- single-serving canned applesauce
- single-serving canned fruit
- single-serving canned fruit juice
- single-serving canned vegetable or tomato juice
- single-serving sugar-free pudding cups
- small boxes of raisins or other dried fruit
- sugar-free instant breakfast drink mix
- sugar-free instant cocoa mix
- sugar-free or regular gelatin mix

PORTION CONTROL IN COOKING AND SERVING

Cooking for one poses many challenges. One of the hardest issues is achieving portion control. Food is not usually packaged in convenient portions for one; therefore, it is easy to overindulge when choosing portions. Why do you have to worry about portion size? You want to provide your body with a predictable pattern (meal scheduling) and quantity (portion size). By watching how much you eat of any one food, you can include more different foods in your meal plan each day. That variety goes a long way in keeping you satisfied and feeling well. Try some of these helpful tips.

- **Use measuring cups**—especially when you're just beginning to learn the true sizes of recommended servings! Mark the levels of liquid servings with tape on one of your usual glasses to serve as a quick guide. Choose small, slender glasses for servings of less than 1/2 cup, and tall, rounder glasses for larger servings to add visual appeal. It doesn't hurt to add ice to a beverage to boost quantity, not calories!

- **Learn how to read labels.** Serving sizes on the food label may not match what's best for your personal meal plan.

- **Be smart about nutritional analysis.** Notice grams of fat and total calories, as well as calories from fat. Fat provides about 9 calories per gram. In the recipes in this book, the final value sometimes varies a little based on the individual food values in the computer database.

- **Check your cookware.** Use small saucepans, skillets, and dishes for cooking and serving, so that small quantities of food cook correctly and your plates seem full at mealtime. Full plates provide visual satisfaction.

- **Serve yourself once.** Fill your plate in the kitchen, then eat in another room and do something more fun than going back for seconds. Try not to eat in front of the television. Television provides a distraction that can lead to overeating.

- **Slow down and chew your food.** Concentrate on how good it tastes, and how happy you are to be feeling great. By chewing your food well, you can increase your feeling of fullness. Start your meal with a crunchy vegetable or fruit salad to begin to chew right.

- **Shop for one.** Buy food items that are packaged in the smallest quantities possible. This may cost a bit more, but is worth the savings in extra calories! Try lunch-bag-size chips or bite-size candy bars.

- **Invest in good food storage containers.** Portion meats and desserts immediately when you get home from the grocery store. This task may take time, but is a great defense against overeating. Take a box of dry breakfast cereal and store each portion in an individual plastic bag. Do the same for crackers and snacks. Remember, you can repackage anything the manufacturer packaged. Do *not* use old food containers for storage, even if you have washed them out—traces of margarine or cottage cheese can remain in the tubs and be a source of cross-contamination.

- **Manage your food cravings.** Everyone has them. You're not a bad person for feeling tempted by food, and your meal plan is not doomed to failure if you find yourself craving something formerly forbidden! Include that food—in moderation and occasionally. Experiment with buying or making new foods in the hope of finding other ways to satisfy yourself. If you like chips, you may find that you also like other crunchy items, such as fresh vegetables, fresh fruit, air-popped popcorn, and whole-grain crackers.

TABLE TIPS

Eating by yourself has some rewards—it's quiet, you don't have to make small talk, and no one objects if you spill something! Eating by yourself can be a pleasant experience. Find ways to make food and the table more appealing. Often when we are alone, we may choose to eat away from the table, on a couch or chair in front of the television. There is nothing wrong with that. However, you may not really be focusing on the meal, and it may not be a source of enjoyment and satisfaction to you. Try some of these tips to add interest to your dining experience.

- **Buy decorated paper plates and napkins.** Who likes to wash dishes? Cleanup has never been anyone's favorite activity, and may add a sense of drudgery to your meal. Paper plates are easy, pretty, and add color and variety to your day. Buy different styles for each season of the year. Enjoy the extra time you don't have to spend washing them! Buy decorated paper napkins when they are on sale in discount stores or card shops—they're a great improvement over torn paper towels!

- **Set the table beautifully.** First, clear it off, especially of bills and chores, which do not create a relaxing atmosphere at your table. Use a beautiful centerpiece, such as fresh wildflowers or herbs, a spring tree branch, an inexpensive scented candle, a favorite family photo, a seashell, fresh fruit, or silk flowers. Put a copy of a new magazine or travel guide nearby for later reading. Change the centerpiece every week. Use single placemats, single cloth napkins, and single place settings you find on sale.

- **Create a mood.** Make the environment during mealtime comforting or fun, whatever your preference. Turn off the television and turn on your favorite music. If you feel tired, enjoy the peaceful silence. Turn on bright lights, or dim them and relax.

- **Cherish your schedule.** Our appetite response is related to our schedules. The more you stay on a schedule, the more regular your appetite response to meals will be. Even if you do not feel like eating a regular meal, try to make an effort to prepare a snack at your usual mealtime.

SHOPPING SMART

Do you dread or enjoy grocery shopping? For many people with diabetes, shopping can be a frustrating task. You don't know what to buy, specialty products are more expensive, and the aisles are full of temptation. The smaller packages you need often cost much more per serving.

Plan in Advance

What can you do? First, plan several days' menus before you go to the store. Then make a shopping list. Post the menus and shopping list on the refrigerator door. Add to the list as you think of items you need. Write your list on the back of an envelope, then fill the envelope with coupons to take to the store. Organize your list according to the store aisles so you'll shop more quickly without backtracking to get missed items. The longer you stay in the store, the more likely it is you'll buy unhealthy foods and spend too much money. Shop when you're not hungry, and you'll avoid compulsively buying food you don't really need.

Cruise the Aisles

What should you buy at the store? Start at the produce section. Stock up on low-fat, high-fiber fruits and vegetables. Fruits are always ideal for quick desserts. Look for fruits and vegetables in season because they'll have the best flavor then. Choose plenty of lettuce, cabbage, carrots, tomatoes, and other vegetables to make into salads. Use the salad bars to buy smaller portions of fruit and vegetable to avoid extra expense and waste.

In the bread section, look for breads that have whole wheat as one of the first ingredients. Many "multigrain" breads have wheat flour as the first ingredient. Wheat flour is just another name for white flour. Ideally, a serving of bread should have two grams or more of fiber per serving. That doesn't mean you should never eat bread made only from white flour, but try to eat whole-grain bread more often. Choose high-fat breads like croissants, muffins, and biscuits sparingly. Read the labels and choose breads that have less than three grams of fat per serving.

Most grocery stores now have fresh fish available in the meat section. Fresh fish is the original fast food. Most can be broiled, boiled, or baked in less than 20 minutes. Use spices and herbs and oils high in monounsaturated fat like olive or canola for flavoring. You may want to stretch your meat and poultry portion with vegetables and starches like brown rice, potatoes, or whole-wheat pasta. Put strips of meat and poultry in stir-frys, stews, soups, and salads— you'll save on money, fat, and calories. Lower-fat choices include beef and pork tenderloin, flank steak, skinless poultry, turkey that is not self-basting, and round steak. If you buy ground white meat of chicken or turkey, be sure the package says that it is at least 95% fat free.

In the dairy section, stock up on low-fat cheeses that have six grams or less of fat per serving. Also, choose dairy products like nonfat milk, sour cream, and yogurt. Make sure your low-fat or nonfat yogurt is plain or sweetened with artificial sweetener. You may want to use whole eggs sparingly—use egg whites (two replace one whole egg) or egg substitute. Buy reduced-fat margarine in a tub or bottle. These spreads are not recommended for baking or sauteing, so use canola or olive oil for those purposes.

Choose Wisely

There are many fat-free and sugar-free baked and frozen desserts on the market for you to choose from. These foods still have calories, however! Enjoy them in moderation, and substitute any carbohydrate they contain for other carbohydrates in your meal plan. Remember, it is the total amount of carbohydrate in each meal and snack that counts.

Other items to have on hand include sugar-free drink mixes; canned fruits packed in their own juices or lite syrup; high-fiber, low-fat, and low-sugar cereals; reduced-sugar fruit spreads; low-fat crackers; low-sodium canned vegetables; whole-grain and enriched pastas; evaporated skim milk; and a generous selection of herbs and spices.

BREAK THE SALT HABIT

Many of us have learned to love salt and salty foods. The typical American diet is high in salt due to the frequent use of processed foods and fast foods. If you have a problem with high blood pressure, use less salt over several weeks to help yourself slowly break the salt habit. This also increases your sensitivity to salt; therefore, you may find you need less salt than before to satisfy you. Or try the following ideas.

- **Use the juice from fresh lemons and limes** on poultry, fish, and vegetables.

- **Buy more herbs and spices!** Try chives, dill, rosemary, tarragon, sage, thyme, oregano, dry mustard, and sage. Remember, many herbs and spices begin to lose their flavor after being exposed to air. Get rid of herbs that have been in your pantry for more than one year. Store herbs in a cool, dry place, not above the stove or near heat and light. Use fresh herbs when you can for the best flavor (use twice as much as dried in most recipes).

- **Try flavored vinegars.** Combine different vinegars with herbs in glass containers that can be sealed tightly. These make great gifts!

READING FOOD LABELS

Many products are labeled "healthy," "diet," and "low-fat." What do these terms really mean? Below is a list that explains them.

- **Free, without, no, or zero**

  The product contains none, or only amounts that would not significantly affect the body. For example, cholesterol-free means that a product has 2 milligrams or less per serving. A food labeled fat-free must have less than 1/2 gram per serving. To be labeled sodium-free, a food must have less than 5 milligrams of sodium per serving. To be called calorie-free, a food must have fewer than 5 calories per serving.

- **Low fat**

  There are 3 grams or less of fat per serving.

- **Low saturated fat**

  There is less than 1 gram of saturated fat per serving.

- **Low sodium**

  There are less than 140 milligrams of sodium per serving.

- **Very low sodium**

  There are less than 35 milligrams of sodium per serving.

- **Low cholesterol**

  There are less than 20 milligrams of cholesterol per serving.

- **Low calorie**

  There are fewer than 40 calories per serving.

- **Lean**

  There are less than 10 grams of fat, less than 4 grams of saturated fat, and less than 95 milligrams of cholesterol in this meat product serving.

- **Extra lean**

  There are less than 5 grams of fat, less than 2 grams of saturated fat, and less than 95 milligrams of cholesterol per serving in this meat product serving.

■ **Light**   Either the product contains 1/3 fewer calories than the regular product, 1/2 the total fat of the regular product, or 1/2 the total sodium of the regular product.

FOOD SAFETY

A major problem for people who live alone or with only one other person is the tendency for food to spoil before it can be used. Watch for two dangers associated with storing food: simple spoilage and bacterial poisoning. The bacteria that cause food spoilage usually give off a terrible smell that clearly indicates the food is bad. With food poisoning, often there is no obvious sign that the food is contaminated until you get sick. The only solution for food poisoning is prevention.

Foods that contain protein are most likely to cause food poisoning, but all foods need to be stored properly. The bacteria that cause food poisoning grow best at temperatures between 40 and 140 degrees—in other words, room temperature. The general rule is that food should not be kept out at room temperature for more than two hours. However, in very warm conditions, like on a sunny beach, two hours may be too long for safety. The best rule of thumb is to serve the food just before you are ready to eat, and immediately store it in shallow covered containers in the refrigerator or iced cooler when the meal is over.

Any leftovers should be eaten within one to three days unless you immediately freeze them. Ideally, you will rotate fresh and packaged goods so that the oldest products are in the front of the refrigerator, freezer, or cupboard. Look for the freshness dates or use-by dates on labels, or date leftovers yourself. Most canned goods are safe for one year. Use raw meat, fish, and poultry within two to three days.

The simplest way to prevent trouble is to wash your hands thoroughly with warm soapy water for 20 seconds. Be sure the towel you use to dry your hands is clean, too. Take particular care when handling raw meat, fish, and poultry. Keep other food away from them, especially if the other food will be served uncooked. Use separate cutting boards, utensils, and serving dishes for raw and cooked foods. Wash cutting boards, utensils, and dishes in hot, soapy water and air-dry them. Change and wash dishcloths and towels often.

This may all sound like common sense, but it's surprising how easy it is to ignore these simple precautions, with sometimes serious consequences. One episode of food poisoning can ruin your blood glucose control for days. Even mild stomach upsets can leave you weak and shaky.

FOOD STORAGE

Since you may buy food in larger packages or prepare some recipes that have more than one or two servings, leftovers may be an issue for you. Here are some guidelines for storing food in your freezer. The key to safe storage is proper dating and marking of food packages so they can be used within a safe time period. Also, check to be sure your freezer is set to the proper temperature.

COMMERCIALLY FROZEN FOOD

Food	Approximate Months in Storage
Frozen fruits and vegetables	
Unsweetened fruits	12
Fruit juice concentrates	12
Vegetables	8
Baked goods	
Bread and rolls	3
Angel food cake	2

COMMERCIALLY FROZEN FOOD (continued)

Food	Approximate Months in Storage
Meat, raw	
Beef roasts and steak	12
Ground beef	4
Lamb	9
Pork, cured	2
Pork, fresh	8
Sausage	2
Veal	9
Meat, cooked	
Meat dinners and pies	3
Poultry, raw	
Chicken and turkey, cut up	6
Chicken and turkey, whole	12
Poultry, cooked	
Chicken and turkey dinners and pies	6
Fried chicken pieces and dinners	3
Fish and shellfish	
Lower-fat fish (cod, flounder, haddock, or halibut)	6
Higher-fat fish (salmon, mullet, trout, or bass)	3
Shrimp, unbreaded	12
Crabmeat	2
Oysters, shucked	1
Fish dinner or fish in sauce	3
Ice cream	1

Foods that are safe to store at room temperature should be placed in cool cabinets away from appliances that produce heat and humidity. Always rotate foods that are older to the front of the cabinet so they can be used first. Never use food in cans that are bulging or packages that are dusty or damaged.

SHELF-STABLE FOOD

Food	Approximate Storage Time
Bouillon cubes or granules	2 years
Canned food, unopened	1 year
Cereals, ready to eat, unopened	6–12 months
Cereals, ready to eat, opened	2–3 months
Cornmeal	1 year
Cornstarch	18 months
Crackers	3 months
Flour, whole wheat or white	6–8 months
Fruit juices, canned, unopened	9 months
Fruit, dried	6 months
Grits, uncooked	1 year
Mayonnaise, unopened	2–3 months
Milk, evaporated, unopened	1 year
nonfat dry, unopened	6 months
nonfat dry, opened	3 months
Nuts, in unopened shell	4 months
shelled, unopened package	3 months
shelled, opened package	2 weeks
Onions	2 weeks
Pancake mix	6–9 months
Pasta, uncooked	2 years
Peas and beans, dried	1 year
Popcorn, unpopped	2 years
Potatoes, white	2–4 weeks
sweet	1–2 weeks
Peanut butter, unopened	6–9 months
opened	2–3 months
Potatoes, instant	6–12 months
Pudding mix	1 year
Rice, uncooked brown or white	2 years

SHELF-STABLE FOOD (continued)

Food	Approximate Storage Time
Salad dressings, unopened	10–12 months
Spices and herbs, ground	6 months
Whole spices	1 year
Vegetable oils, unopened	6 months
opened	1–3 months

Foods stored in the refrigerator need to be used quickly for the best quality and safety. Mark each storage container with labels describing what is inside and when it was prepared. Clean out your refrigerator at least every two weeks.

REFRIGERATED FOOD

Food	Maximum Storage Times
Dairy products	
Milk	5–7 days after date on carton
Hard cheese	6 months
Cottage cheese	3 days
Other soft cheeses	7 days
Butter	2 weeks
Eggs	
Whole, fresh	3 weeks
Hard cooked	1 week
Liquid substitutes	
opened	3 days
unopened	10 days

REFRIGERATED FOOD (continued)

Food	Maximum Storage Time
Fresh meat	
Ground beef and stew meat	1–2 days
Beef roasts, steaks	3–5 days
Fresh pork	3–5 days
Fresh lamb	3–5 days
Variety meats like liver, kidney, or tongue	1–2 days
Cooked Meat	
Cooked meat and meat dishes	3–4 days
Gravy and meat broth	1–2 days
Cured Meat	
Ham	7 days
whole	3–4 days
sliced	3–5 days
unopened canned	7 days
Bacon	7 days
Sausage	
raw bulk	1–2 days
smoked patties or links	7 days
pepperoni or jerky	2–3 weeks
Lunch meats	
opened	3–5 days
unopened	2 weeks
Hot dogs	
opened	1 week
unopened	2 weeks
Fresh poultry	
Whole chicken or turkey	1–2 days
Poultry pieces	1–2 days

REFRIGERATED FOOD (continued)

Food	Maximum Storage Times
Cooked poultry	
Cooked poultry dishes	3–4 days
Pieces	3–4 days
Pieces covered with broth or gravy	1–2 days
Fish and seafood	
Fin fish	1–2 days
Shell fish	2–3 days
Meat, chicken, or fish salads	3–5 days
Soups or stews, with or without meat	3–4 days
Fruits	
Apples	2 weeks
Berries and cherries	2–5 days
Citrus	1 month
Grapes	3–5 days
Pears	3–5 days
Plums	1 week
Vegetables	
Cabbage	2 weeks
Other fresh vegetables	5 days

Quick
Breakfasts

Bagel Sandwich

Preparation Time: 3 minutes

Good for breakfast, lunch, or a filling snack to keep on the go!

- 2 oz reduced-fat cream cheese
- 1 Tbsp chopped golden raisins
- 1 Tbsp chopped pitted dates
- 1 Tbsp chopped walnuts
- 1 tsp unsweetened pineapple or orange juice
- 1 sesame seed bagel, halved and toasted

Combine the cream cheese, raisins, dates, walnuts, and pineapple juice in a small bowl and mix well. Spread the filling on the toasted bagel halves and serve.

Serves 1

Exchanges

3 Starch
1 Fruit
3 Fat

Calories 446
 Calories from Fat . .164
Total Fat . . . . .18 g
 Saturated Fat . . . . . . .9 g
Cholesterol . . . . .40 mg
Sodium . . . . .627 mg
Carbohydrate . . . . . .57 g
 Dietary Fiber . . . . . . .3 g
 Sugars . . . . .18 g
Protein . . . . .15 g

Breakfast to Go!

Preparation Time: 10 minutes

Enjoy this fast shake in your auto mug while you drive to work.

1/2 cup sliced bananas

1 cup nonfat milk

1/2 cup plain nonfat yogurt

1/4 cup 100% bran flakes

1 tsp vanilla extract

2 tsp sugar

1/2 cup ice

Dash cinnamon or nutmeg

1. Combine all ingredients in a blender and process on medium speed until smooth. Garnish with cinnamon or nutmeg.

2. You can substitute strawberries, peaches, or other fresh fruit for the bananas if you like.

Serves 1

Exchanges

1 Starch
1 Fruit
1 1/2 Skim Milk

Calories 275
  Calories from Fat . . . 10
Total Fat . . . . 1 g
  Saturated Fat . . . . . . 0 g
Cholesterol . . . . 7 mg
Sodium . . . . 313 mg
Carbohydrate . . . . . . 55 g
  Dietary Fiber . . . . . 8 g
  Sugars . . . . 37 g
Protein . . . . 18 g

Cinnamon Toast Bagels

Preparation Time: 3 minutes

A quick version of an old favorite—spicy cinnamon on a chewy bagel!

1 whole-wheat bagel, halved

1 Tbsp low-calorie margarine

2 dashes ground cinnamon

2 tsp sugar

Spread the margarine on the bagel halves and sprinkle with cinnamon and sugar. Toast as desired on a tray in a toaster oven or regular oven.

Serves 1

Exchanges

3 Starch
2 Fat

Calories 278
  Calories from Fat 61
Total Fat . . . . 7 g
  Saturated Fat . . . . . . 1 g
Cholesterol . . . . 0 mg
Sodium . . . . 470 mg
Carbohydrate . . . . . . 46 g
  Dietary Fiber . . . . 2 g
  Sugars . . . . 11 g
Protein . . . . 7 g

Fiber-Rich French Toast

Preparation Time: 15 minutes

A hearty way to start the day!

1/4 cup liquid egg substitute

1/4 cup nonfat milk

1/8 tsp vanilla extract

1/4 tsp ground cinnamon

1/2 tsp brown sugar

  2 slices whole-grain bread

  1 tsp chopped pecans

1. Preheat a medium nonstick skillet over medium heat. Mix together the egg substitute, milk, vanilla, cinnamon, and brown sugar in a small, wide-mouth bowl (a soup plate works best).

2. Dip the bread in the egg mixture, coating both sides. Place the bread in the skillet and cook until both sides are brown, turning with a spatula.

3. Place the toast on a serving plate and sprinkle with chopped pecans. Top with sugar-free syrup or all-fruit preserves and serve immediately.

Serves 1

Exchanges

2 Starch
1 Very Lean Meat

Calories 214
  Calories from Fat . . . 32
Total Fat . . . . 4 g
  Saturated Fat . . . . . . 1 g
Cholesterol . . . . 1 mg
Sodium . . . . 437 mg
Carbohydrate . . . . . . 33 g
  Dietary Fiber . . . . 4 g
  Sugars . . . . 8 g
Protein . . . . 14 g

Hearty Lumberjack Pancakes

Preparation Time: 10 minutes

Make this recipe the night before for best results.

1/4 cup quick-cooking oats

1/2 cup all-purpose flour

1 Tbsp brown sugar

1 tsp baking powder

1/4 tsp allspice

1/4 tsp cinnamon

1/2 cup nonfat milk

1 Tbsp canola oil

1/4 tsp vanilla extract

1/4 cup liquid egg substitute

1. Combine the oats, flour, brown sugar, baking powder, and spices in a medium storage container with a lid.

2. Whisk together the milk, oil, vanilla, and liquid egg substitute and pour into the oat mixture. Stir well until the mixture is uniform in consistency. Do not overmix. Cover and chill for at least 1 hour, or overnight.

3. Preheat a nonstick griddle or skillet over medium-high heat. Pour 1/4 cup of the batter onto the griddle for each pancake. Cook until bubbles appear on top of pancakes. Flip with a nonstick spatula and continue cooking until light brown.

4. Top with fresh fruit or sugar-free syrup and serve immediately.

Serves 2
Exchanges

3 Starch
1 Monounsaturated Fat

Calories 283
  Calories from Fat . . . 72
Total Fat . . . . 8 g
  Saturated Fat . . . . . . 1 g
Cholesterol . . . . 1 mg
Sodium . . . . 272 mg
Carbohydrate . . . . . . 42 g
  Dietary Fiber . . . . . . 2 g
  Sugars . . . . 11 g
Protein . . . . 10 g

Lemon Charge

Preparation Time: 12 minutes

Serve as a snack or a breakfast drink.

1/4 cup fresh strawberries, washed and sliced

2 tsp sugar (optional)

1/2 cup nonfat milk

4 oz artificially sweetened, lemon-flavored, low-fat yogurt

Using a blender or food processor, blend the strawberries and sugar together. Slowly pour in the milk and yogurt and blend until frothy. Garnish with a lemon slice or a sliced strawberry.

Serves 1

Exchanges

2 Carbohydrate

Calories 181
  Calories from Fat . . . 16
Total Fat . . . . 2 g
  Saturated Fat . . . . . . 1 g
Cholesterol . . . . 7 mg
Sodium . . . . 136 mg
Carbohydrate . . . . . . 32 g
  Dietary Fiber . . . . . . 1 g
  Sugars . . . . 29 g
Protein . . . . 9 g

Luscious Cheese Toast

Preparation Time: 4 minutes

A snack? A breakfast item? A brunch item? You decide!

3 Tbsp 1% low-fat cottage cheese

1/8 tsp almond extract

2 tsp sugar

1 Tbsp low-sugar apricot jam (or flavor of choice)

1 slice whole-wheat bread

1. Using a food processor or blender, combine the cottage cheese, almond extract, sugar, and jam. Lightly toast the bread and spread it with the cottage cheese mixture.

2. Place the toast on a baking tray and broil until the cheese begins to brown lightly.

Serves 1

Exchanges

2 Carbohydrate

Calories 153
  Calories from Fat . . . 14
Total Fat . . . . 2 g
  Saturated Fat . . . . . 1 g
Cholesterol . . . . 4 mg
Sodium . . . . 287 mg
Carbohydrate . . . . . 28 g
  Dietary Fiber . . . . . . 2 g
  Sugars . . . . 13 g
Protein . . . . 8 g

Morning Rush-Hour Burrito

Preparation Time: 5 minutes

This breakfast travels well in rush-hour traffic.

1 Tbsp reduced-fat cream cheese

1 6-inch flour tortilla

1 tsp strawberry jam

1 New Zealand kiwi fruit, peeled and thinly sliced

1. Spread the cream cheese over the flour tortilla. Spread the strawberry jam over half of the tortilla.

2. Place the kiwi slices over the other half of the tortilla. Fold the two sides together and serve.

Serves 1

Exchanges
1 Starch
1 1/2 Fruit
1 Fat

Calories 211
  Calories from Fat . . . 51
Total Fat . . . . 6 g
  Saturated Fat . . . . . . 2 g
Cholesterol . . . . 10 mg
Sodium . . . . 220 mg
Carbohydrate . . . . . . 36 g
  Dietary Fiber . . . . 4 g
  Sugars . . . . 14 g
Protein . . . . 5 g

Omelet Mexicano

Preparation Time: 3 minutes

Tastes great any time of the day!

1/2 cup liquid egg substitute

1 Tbsp nonfat milk

2 Tbsp canned, prepared chili beans

1 Tbsp chopped onion

1 Tbsp nonfat sour cream

1 Tbsp prepared salsa

1. Spray a small skillet or omelet pan with non-stick cooking spray and preheat over medium-high heat.

2. Whisk together the egg substitute and milk in a small bowl. Pour the egg mixture into the hot skillet. When the egg mixture begins to solidify, lift it along the edges to allow the uncooked liquid to flow underneath for even cooking. Be sure to use a nonstick spatula.

3. When the egg mixture is completely firm, form it into a circle. Spread the prepared chili on half of the circle and sprinkle the chopped onion on top. Fold the egg mixture over to form the omelet.

4. Reduce the heat to medium and cover. Continue cooking for about 2 minutes or until the contents are thoroughly hot. Top with sour cream and salsa.

Serves 1

Exchanges
1 Carbohydrate
2 Very Lean Meat

Calories 127
  Calories from Fat 2
Total Fat . . . . 0 g
  Saturated Fat . . . . . . 0 g
Cholesterol . . . . 0 mg
Sodium . . . . 394 mg
Carbohydrate . . . . . . 13 g
  Dietary Fiber . . . . 3 g
  Sugars . . . . 6 g
Protein . . . . 16 g

Quick Sticky Muffins

Preparation Time: 19 minutes

These muffins are delicious with hot coffee and fresh fruit.

2 Tbsp sugar-free, maple-flavored syrup

4 tsp chopped pecans

3/4 cup reduced-fat baking mix

1/4 tsp cinnamon

1/4 tsp vanilla extract

2 dashes allspice

1 tsp margarine, melted

1 tsp sugar

1/2 cup nonfat milk

1. Preheat the oven to 375 degrees. Spray 4 compartments of a muffin tin with nonstick cooking spray.

2. Spoon 1/2 Tbsp maple syrup into each muffin compartment and sprinkle 1 tsp chopped pecans in each.

3. Combine the remaining ingredients in a small mixing bowl until the ingredients are well moistened. Spoon the batter into the muffin compartments until each is half full.

4. Bake for 15–17 minutes or until the muffins are puffed and lightly brown. Cool for 1 minute, then invert the muffin pan on a sheet of waxed paper to allow the muffins to fall out.

Serves 2

Exchanges

2 1/2 Starch
1 Fat

Calories 253
  Calories from Fat . . . 67
Total Fat . . . . 7 g
  Saturated Fat . . . . . . 1 g
Cholesterol . . . . 2 mg
Sodium . . . . 603 mg
Carbohydrate . . . . . 40 g
  Dietary Fiber . . . . 1 g
  Sugars . . . . 9 g
Protein . . . . 6 g

Summary Cooler

Preparation Time: 3 minutes

This is a refreshing breakfast drink or snack.

1 small banana, peeled and sliced

1/3 cup low-calorie cranberry juice cocktail

1/2 cup crushed ice

1 cup sugar-free tonic water

1. Combine the banana, cranberry juice, and ice in a blender and process until smooth.

2. Slowly add the tonic water and stir to blend. Serve at once.

Serves 1

Exchanges

1 1/2 Fruit

Calories 77
  Calories from Fat 3
Total Fat . . . . 0 g
  Saturated Fat . . . . . . 0 g
Cholesterol . . . . 0 mg
Sodium . . . . 47 mg
Carbohydrate . . . . . . 20 g
  Dietary Fiber . . . . 2 g
  Sugars . . . . 14 g
Protein . . . . 1 g

Speedy Salads

Cactus Salad Dressing

Preparation Time: 5 minutes

Try this spicy dressing on salads, as a dip for fresh vegetables, or as a sauce for grilled steak or chicken.

- 1 cup plain nonfat yogurt
- 4 Tbsp coarse Dijon-style mustard
- 5 tsp vinegar
- 1 tsp onion powder
- 4 dashes hot pepper sauce
- 3 drops green food coloring

Combine all ingredients in a small glass container and mix well. Refrigerate and use within 1 week.

Serves 12

Serving Size: 2 Tbsp

Exchanges

Free Food

Calories	15
Calories from Fat	2
Total Fat	0 g
Saturated Fat	0 g
Cholesterol	0 mg
Sodium	80 mg
Carbohydrate	2 g
Dietary Fiber	0 g
Sugars	2 g
Protein	1 g

Colorful Macaroni Salad

Preparation Time: 15 minutes

Here's a cold macaroni salad for a hot summer day!

1/4 cup liquid egg substitute

1 1/2 Tbsp plain nonfat yogurt

1 1/2 Tbsp lite mayonnaise

1 tsp sugar

1/2 cup diced celery

2 Tbsp chopped green onions

2 Tbsp chopped red bell peppers

1 small carrot, grated

1 cup small whole-wheat macaroni, cooked and well drained

Fresh ground black pepper to taste

Dash sweet paprika

1. Place the egg substitute in a small microwavable bowl, cover with plastic wrap, and microwave on high for 30 seconds. Let it cool slightly, and cut it into small pieces with a table knife.

2. Mix together the yogurt, mayonnaise, and sugar in a small mixing bowl. Add the vegetables, cooked macaroni, and egg substitute pieces and mix well. Cover the bowl and chill for at least 2 hours.

3. Season with pepper and paprika and serve.

Serves 1

Exchanges

3 Starch
2 Vegetable

Calories 289
  Calories from Fat . . . 9
Total Fat . . . . 1 g
  Saturated Fat . . . . . . 0 g
Cholesterol . . . . 0 mg
Sodium . . . . 361 mg
Carbohydrate . . . . . . 56 g
  Dietary Fiber . . . . 9 g
  Sugars . . . . 14 g
Protein . . . . 17 g

Cucumber and Sprout Salad

Preparation Time: 10 minutes

If you're short on time, get all the ingredients for this quick salad from the salad bar at the grocery store.

1/2 cup red leaf lettuce, washed, dried, and torn

1 cup Boston lettuce, washed, dried, and torn

1/2 cup alfalfa sprouts

1 whole small cucumber, peeled, sliced and quartered

2 sprigs fresh cilantro, chopped

1 Tbsp dry-roasted sunflower seeds

Combine all ingredients, top with your favorite dressing, and serve.

Serves 2

Exchanges

1 Vegetable
1/2 Polyunsaturated Fat

Calories 41
  Calories from Fat . . . 20
Total Fat . . . . 2 g
  Saturated Fat . . . . . . 0 g
Cholesterol . . . . 0 mg
Sodium . . . . 5 mg
Carbohydrate . . . . 4 g
  Dietary Fiber . . . . 2 g
  Sugars . . . . 2 g
Protein . . . . 2 g

Far East Salad

Preparation Time: 15 minutes

You'll enjoy this crunchy, flavorful salad.

1	cup shredded lettuce
1/2	cup coarsely chopped fresh broccoli
1/2	cup fresh snow peas (if frozen, thaw)
1/4	cup shredded carrot
1/4	cup canned sliced water chestnuts
1/4	whole green or red bell pepper, cut into strips
1/2	cup fresh bean sprouts
1	Tbsp canola oil
1	tsp lemon juice
1 1/2	tsp sesame oil
1	tsp lite soy sauce
1/4	tsp ground ginger
2	tsp sugar

1. Arrange the shredded lettuce to cover a dinner plate. In layers, add the broccoli, snow peas, carrots, water chestnuts, bell pepper, and bean sprouts.

2. Whisk together the remaining ingredients and pour the dressing over the salad.

Serves 1

Exchanges

2 Carbohydrate
4 Monounsaturated Fat

Calories 328
  Calories from Fat . . .194
Total Fat . . . . 22 g
  Saturated Fat . . . . . . 2 g
Cholesterol . . . . 0 mg
Sodium . . . . 237 mg
Carbohydrate . . . . . . 32 g
  Dietary Fiber . . . . . . 8 g
  Sugars . . . . 20 g
Protein . . . . 7 g

Favorite Carrot Raisin Salad

Preparation Time: 10 minutes

This tasty and colorful salad is full of vitamin A and is a good source of fiber.

1 large carrot, peeled and grated

2 Tbsp raisins

1 Tbsp plain nonfat yogurt

2 Tbsp crushed pineapple, canned in its own juice

1 Tbsp lite mayonnaise

2 tsp sugar

1. Combine all the ingredients in a small bowl and mix well.

2. Refrigerate for at least 1 hour before serving.

Serves 2

Exchanges

1 1/2 Carbohydrate

Calories 91
  Calories from Fat . . . 2
Total Fat . . . . 0 g
  Saturated Fat . . . . . . 0 g
Cholesterol . . . . 0 mg
Sodium . . . . 85 mg
Carbohydrate . . . . . . 22 g
  Dietary Fiber . . . . 3 g
  Sugars . . . . 18 g
Protein . . . . 2 g

Garlic Dill Dressing

Preparation Time: 10 minutes

Great as a salad dressing or on fish instead of tartar sauce!

1/2 cup reduced-fat cream cheese

1/4 cup plain nonfat yogurt

1/4 cup chopped green onions

1/2 tsp garlic powder

1/2 tsp dried dill weed

3 Tbsp chopped dill pickle

2 tsp lemon juice

2 tsp Worcestershire sauce

1. Using a blender or mixer, puree the cream cheese and yogurt together until smooth. Add the remaining ingredients and blend for 1 minute. If the mixture is too thick, thin with 1 tsp lemon juice or water.

2. Refrigerate in a covered container. Shake well before serving.

Serves 8
Serving Size: 1 Tbsp
Exchanges
1 Saturated Fat

Calories 42
  Calories from Fat . . . 27
Total Fat . . . . 3 g
  Saturated Fat . . . . . . 2 g
Cholesterol . . . . 10 mg
Sodium . . . . 126 mg
Carbohydrate . . . . 2 g
  Dietary Fiber . . . . 0 g
  Sugars . . . . 1 g
Protein . . . . 2 g

Honey-Mustard Chicken Salad

Preparation Time: 10 minutes

Use canned chicken to make this fast, colorful salad.

4 oz canned low-sodium white chicken, drained

1/4 tsp grated fresh lemon peel

2 Tbsp fat-free honey-mustard salad dressing

1/4 cup chopped water chestnuts

1/2 cup sliced, seedless red grapes

1 cup fresh spinach, washed, dried, and stems removed

1 tsp pine nuts

Fresh ground pepper to taste

1. Toss the chicken, lemon peel, salad dressing, water chestnuts, and grapes together in a small bowl until all ingredients are lightly coated.

2. Let the salad stand for 5 minutes to absorb the dressing. Meanwhile, toast the pine nuts for 2 minutes in a nonstick skillet over medium heat, shaking the pan constantly.

3. Arrange the spinach on a plate. Place the salad on top of the spinach. Sprinkle the pine nuts on top, add pepper to taste, and serve.

Serves 1

Exchanges
2 Carbohydrate
4 Very Lean Meat
1/2 Fat

Calories 274
  Calories from Fat . . . 47
Total Fat . . . . 5 g
  Saturated Fat . . . . . . 1 g
Cholesterol . . . . 60 mg
Sodium . . . . 359 mg
Carbohydrate . . . . . . 32 g
  Dietary Fiber . . . . 3 g
  Sugars . . . . 23 g
Protein . . . . 29 g

Kathleen's Croutons

Preparation Time: 4 minutes

Use these crunchy croutons as a topping for salads, soups, and stews, or eat them as a snack.

1 slice white bread

1 slice whole-wheat bread

   Onion powder

   Garlic powder

   Dried thyme

   Red pepper

   Dried oregano

   Sweet paprika

   Dried parsley

   Cajun spice blend (optional)

1 tsp taco or chili seasoning mix (optional)

1. Preheat the oven to 300 degrees. Cut the bread into 1/2-inch cubes and place in a small bowl.

2. Spray the bread cubes with nonstick cooking spray, coating each side lightly. Sprinkle the bread cubes with herbs and spices as desired. (For spicier croutons, use Cajun spices or taco seasoning; for a milder flavor, use parsley, onion powder, and sweet paprika.)

3. Spray a baking sheet with nonstick cooking spray. Spread the cubes on a tray to form one layer. Toast the bread cubes in a conventional or toaster oven. Stir the bread cubes frequently to toast all sides as evenly as possible.

4. Remove the pan from the oven and allow the croutons to cool. Store in an air-tight container.

Serves 4

Serving Size: 1/4 cup

Exchanges

1/2 Starch

Calories 34
  Calories from Fat . . . 5
Total Fat . . . . 1 g
  Saturated Fat . . . . . . 0 g
Cholesterol . . . . 0 mg
Sodium . . . . 71 mg
Carbohydrate . . . . 6 g
  Dietary Fiber . . . . 1 g
  Sugars . . . . 1 g
Protein . . . . 1 g

Luncheon Spinach Salad

Preparation Time: 3 minutes

Strawberries and vinegar? Try it!

1 cup spinach leaves, washed, drained, and torn

1 oz reduced-fat cream cheese, chilled

1/2 cup sliced fresh strawberries

1 Tbsp slivered, toasted almonds

1 tsp balsamic vinegar

1 tsp extra-virgin olive oil

1. Arrange the spinach leaves on a plate.

2. Pinch off pieces of cream cheese and roll into small balls, each about the size of a pea (cold cream cheese works best).

3. Spoon the sliced berries and cream cheese balls onto the spinach leaves. Sprinkle with almonds, drizzle with vinegar and oil, and serve.

Serves 1

Exchanges
1/2 Carbohydrate
3 Fat

Calories 188
  Calories from Fat . . .132
Total Fat . . . . 15 g
  Saturated Fat . . . . . . 5 g
Cholesterol . . . . 20 mg
Sodium . . . . 166 mg
Carbohydrate . . . . . . 11 g
  Dietary Fiber . . . . 4 g
  Sugars . . . . 6 g
Protein . . . . 6 g

Mardi Gras Potato Salad

Preparation Time: 40 minutes

This colorful salad will add interest to your meal as a side dish.

2 small red potatoes, unpeeled

2 Tbsp plain nonfat yogurt

2 Tbsp lite mayonnaise

1/2 tsp celery seed

1/4 tsp dry mustard

2 Tbsp red wine vinegar

2 tsp sugar

1/4 cup chopped celery

1/4 cup chopped red bell peppers

1 small carrot, shredded

2 Tbsp chopped onions

Dash white pepper

Dash sweet paprika

4 lettuce leaves

1. Boil the red potatoes in water for about 15 minutes or microwave on high for 8–10 minutes. Let cool.

2. Mix together the yogurt, mayonnaise, celery seed, dry mustard, vinegar, and sugar in a medium bowl.

3. Dice the cooled potatoes and add to the yogurt mixture. Add the remaining ingredients and stir gently until well coated.

4. Refrigerate for at least 1 hour. (For best flavor, refrigerate overnight.) Serve on lettuce leaves.

Serves 2
Exchanges
1 1/2 Starch
1 Vegetable

Calories 134
  Calories from Fat . . . 3
Total Fat . . . . 0 g
  Saturated Fat . . . . . . 0 g
Cholesterol . . . . 0 mg
Sodium . . . . 146 mg
Carbohydrate . . . . . . 31 g
  Dietary Fiber . . . . 3 g
  Sugars . . . . 12 g
Protein . . . . 3 g

Middle Eastern Salad

Preparation Time: 10 minutes

Enjoy this salad as a hearty meal for lunch, or split the recipe into 2 servings and use as side dishes. To cook the couscous, add 1/2 cup boiling water to 1/4 cup dry couscous. Let stand, covered, for 10 minutes until the water is absorbed.

1/2	cup cooked couscous
1/2	cup garbanzo beans, rinsed and drained
2	Tbsp diced celery
3	Tbsp diced red bell pepper
1	small carrot, shredded
1	Tbsp raisins
1 1/2	Tbsp fat-free Italian dressing
4	tsp sugar
	Fresh ground pepper to taste
	Dash dried oregano
4–6	lettuce leaves

Combine all the ingredients except the lettuce in a medium bowl and mix well. Cover and refrigerate for 1 hour. When ready, serve on a bed of lettuce leaves.

Serves 1

Exchanges

4 Starch
2 Vegetable

Calories 364
  Calories from Fat . . . 23
Total Fat . . . . 3 g
  Saturated Fat . . . . . . 0 g
Cholesterol . . . . 0 mg
Sodium . . . . 392 mg
Carbohydrate . . . . . . 76 g
  Dietary Fiber . . . . . . 9 g
  Sugars . . . . 34 g
Protein . . . . 12 g

Soups & Stews

Autumn Harvest Pumpkin Soup

Preparation Time: 15 minutes

This hearty soup is good any time of the year!

1 tsp extra-virgin olive oil

1/4 cup chopped sweet onion

1 cup canned solid-pack pumpkin

1 tomato, chopped and seeded

1/4 cup low-fat, low-sodium chicken broth

Dash salt

Fresh ground pepper to taste

1/2 cup evaporated skim milk, warmed

Dash nutmeg

1. Heat the oil in a small saucepan over medium-high heat. When moderately hot, add the onion and saute until tender.

2. Add the pumpkin, tomato, broth, salt, and pepper. Cover and cook for 8–10 minutes, stirring frequently to blend.

3. Remove the saucepan from the heat. Carefully pour the hot mixture into a blender, using a ladle, and puree until smooth.

4. Gradually add the milk and blend well. Heat again if not warmed enough after blending. Sprinkle with nutmeg before serving.

Serves 2

Exchanges

1 1/2 Starch
1/2 Monounsaturated Fat

Calories 139
  Calories from Fat . . . 29
Total Fat . . . . 3 g
  Saturated Fat . . . . . 1 g
Cholesterol . . . . 2 mg
Sodium . . . . 170 mg
Carbohydrate . . . . . . 23 g
  Dietary Fiber . . . . . . 4 g
  Sugars . . . . 13 g
Protein . . . . 7 g

Cream of Cauliflower Soup

Preparation Time: 22 minutes

This low-calorie vegetable can be made into a delicious and filling soup. Make extra for a delicious casserole (see recipe, p. 41).

8 oz low-fat, low-sodium, condensed cream of chicken soup

1 cup finely chopped cauliflower

1 tsp lemon juice

1 carrot, diced

1/4 tsp black pepper

1/4 tsp dried dill weed

1. Combine all the ingredients in a small saucepan and bring to a boil. Reduce the heat, cover, and simmer for 20 minutes, or until the cauliflower is soft, stirring occasionally.

2. For a thicker soup, blend half of it and mix back into the original.

Serves 2

Exchanges

1 Carbohydrate

Calories 71
  Calories from Fat . . . 12
Total Fat . . . . 1 g
  Saturated Fat . . . . . .0 g
Cholesterol . . . . 4 mg
Sodium . . . . 242 mg
Carbohydrate . . . . . . 13 g
  Dietary Fiber . . . . . . 3 g
  Sugars . . . . 4 g
Protein . . . . 3 g

Fast Stew with Dumplings*

Preparation Time: 3 minutes

Use canned, single-serving, chunky-style soup in this quick and hearty stew.

1 10-oz can chunky vegetable soup (ready to serve)

1/2 cup low-fat all-purpose baking mix

1/4 cup nonfat milk

1/2 tsp dried parsley

1. Prepare the soup as directed and bring to a boil.

2. Combine the baking mix, milk, and parsley in a small bowl. The dough should be heavy and sticky. Add more or less milk to achieve the correct consistency.

3. Drop the dough by heaping tablespoons into the boiling soup. Space the dumplings so they are not crowded.

4. Reduce the heat to medium and cook for 5–7 minutes. Cover and cook for 5–7 more minutes or until the dumplings are firm and puffy.

* This recipe is extremely high in sodium!

Serves 1

Exchanges
4 1/2 Starch
1 Vegetable
1/2 Fat

Calories 409
  Calories from Fat . . . 71
Total Fat . . . . 8 g
  Saturated Fat . . . . . . 2 g
Cholesterol . . . . 2 mg
Sodium . . . . 1819 mg
Carbohydrate . . . . . . 73 g
  Dietary Fiber . . . . 6 g
  Sugars . . . . 12 g
Protein . . . . 11 g

Gulf Breeze Stew*

Preparation Time: 45 minutes

Serve this stew with a slice of fresh cornbread or sourdough bread.

2 cups low-fat, low-sodium chicken broth

1/2 ear frozen corn

3 new potatoes, halved

1/2 cup diced tomatoes

1 clove garlic, minced

1/2 tsp seafood seasoning blend

2 dashes ground cayenne pepper

Fresh ground pepper to taste

1 tsp dried parsley

4 large fresh shrimp, peeled and deveined

1/3 cup sliced turkey kielbasa sausage

1 tsp lemon juice (optional)

1. Heat the chicken broth over medium heat in a medium saucepan. Add the remaining ingredients and bring to a boil.

2. Reduce the heat to simmer and allow to cook for 30 minutes, or until the liquid is reduced by about 1/3 and the potatoes are cooked through. (This stew has a thin consistency.)

Note: If you're using frozen shrimp, defrost and peel before adding to the stew, or pour boiling water over them, let cool, and then peel. Add previously frozen cooked shrimp 5 minutes before serving to prevent overcooking.

* This recipe is high in sodium!

Serves 1

Exchanges

3 Starch
2 Very Lean Meat

Calories 326
  Calories from Fat . . 48
Total Fat . . . . 5 g
  Saturated Fat . . . . . . 2 g
Cholesterol . . . . 134 mg
Sodium . . . . 934 mg
Carbohydrate . . . . . . 49 g
  Dietary Fiber . . . . 5 g
  Sugars . . . . 10 g
Protein . . . . 22 g

Gumbo Baton Rouge

Preparation Time: 15 minutes

This gumbo has lots of ingredients, but it's worth the effort!

1	whole chicken leg, skin removed
1 1/2	Tbsp all-purpose flour
1/4	cup chopped sweet onion
1/4	cup chopped celery
1/4	cup chopped red bell pepper
1	cube low-sodium chicken bouillon
1/4	tsp cayenne pepper
1/8	tsp ground white pepper
1	Tbsp dried parsley
1/8	tsp dried thyme
6	drops Louisiana-style hot sauce
1/3	cup frozen okra
1 oz	turkey kielbasa, sliced into bite-sized pieces
1/4	cup red beans, rinsed and drained
1/2	cup instant, cooked brown rice

1. Place the chicken leg in a small saucepan and add enough fresh water to cover (about 2 cups). Bring to a boil and simmer until the meat falls off the bone. Remove from heat and let cool.

2. Cut the meat into small pieces, removing fat, skin, and bone. Remove any fat from the broth with a ladle, spoon, or paper towel and set the broth aside. Keep the meat refrigerated until ready for use.

3. Heat a large heavy skillet over medium heat. Sprinkle the flour evenly in the skillet and heat until the flour browns. Quickly add the onion,

(continued)

Serves 2

Exchanges

1 1/2 Starch
1 Vegetable
1 Lean Meat

Calories	197
Calories from Fat	35
Total Fat	4 g
Saturated Fat	1 g
Cholesterol	29 mg
Sodium	232 mg
Carbohydrate	28 g
Dietary Fiber	4 g
Sugars	4 g
Protein	13 g

Gumbo Baton Rouge

(*continued*)

celery, bell pepper, and 1 cup of the defatted chicken broth to the skillet, stirring constantly.

3. Add the chicken bouillon cube, cayenne pepper, white pepper, parsley, thyme, hot sauce, and okra. Bring to a boil, then reduce the heat and simmer for 10 minutes.

4. Add the kielbasa, beans, and chicken to the skillet. Stir in the rice and cook for 5 minutes before serving.

Instant Potato Soup

Preparation Time: 15 minutes

Wondering what to do with those leftover mashed potatoes? Fix this soup and a quick salad, and you're ready to eat!

1 Tbsp all-purpose flour

1 tsp low-calorie margarine

1/4 cup chopped white onion

1/2 cup leftover mashed potatoes

1/2 cup low-fat, low-sodium chicken broth

2/3 cup nonfat milk

1/4 tsp white pepper

1 tsp dried chives

1. Combine the flour and margarine in a small saucepan over medium heat. Stir with a wisk to make smooth. Add the onions and stir for 1 minute.

2. Alternately add the potatoes and broth until thick and sticky. Slowly whisk the milk into the mixture until smooth.

3. Reduce the heat and add the pepper and chives. Simmer for 5 minutes and serve hot.

Serves 1

Exchanges

2 1/2 Carbohydrate
1 1/2 Fat

Calories 272
  Calories from Fat . . . 101
Total Fat . . . . 11 g
  Saturated Fat . . . . . . 5 g
Cholesterol . . . . 18 mg
Sodium . . . . 532 mg
Carbohydrate . . . . . . 36 g
  Dietary Fiber . . . . 3 g
  Sugars . . . . 13 g
Protein . . . . .11 g

Tasty Poultry

Cauliflower Casserole

Preparation Time: 5 minutes

Try this delicious home-style casserole with a fresh green salad.

1 cup Cream of Cauliflower
  Soup (see recipe, p. 32)

1 cup cooked egg noodles

4 oz cooked chicken, diced

1/4 cup chopped celery

1/4 cup frozen peas

1/2 tsp onion powder

  Fine dry bread crumbs

1. Preheat the oven to 350 degrees. Place all the ingredients except the bread crumbs in a small, greased casserole dish.

2. Top with the bread crumbs and bake for 20 minutes, or until hot and bubbly.

Serves 2

Exchanges

2 Starch
2 Lean Meat

Calories 267
  Calories from Fat . . 59
Total Fat . . . . 7 g
  Saturated Fat . . . . . . 2 g
Cholesterol . . . . 81 mg
Sodium . . . . 268 mg
Carbohydrate . . . . . . 28 g
  Dietary Fiber . . . . 3 g
  Sugars . . . . 3 g
Protein . . . . 22 g

Chicken Dippers

Preparation Time: 15 minutes

These seasoned chicken chunks are delicious dipped in a variety of sauces.

1/3 cup dry bread crumbs

1/8 tsp white pepper

1/8 tsp black pepper

1/4 tsp marjoram

1/4 tsp onion powder

1/2 tsp dried parsley

1/4 tsp paprika

1 egg white

2 tsp extra-virgin olive oil

1 4 oz skinless, boneless chicken breast, cut into 2-inch pieces

2 Tbsp fat-free Ranch dressing (or other dressing of choice)

1. Mix the bread crumbs and spices in a small shallow bowl. In a separate bowl, beat the egg white with a fork or small wire whisk until light foam appears.

2. Heat the oil in small skillet over medium heat. Dip the chicken chunks into the egg white, dredge them in the bread crumb mixture, and place them on a small plate.

3. Using tongs, carefully place the breaded chicken chunks into the skillet. Turn the pieces when the chicken is thoroughly browned and firm, approximately 3–5 minutes on each side.

4. Drain the chicken on a paper towel. To serve, pour the dressing into a small cup or bowl, dip the chicken, and enjoy.

Serves 1

Exchanges

2 1/2 Starch
4 Lean Meat

Calories 428
  Calories from Fat . 127
Total Fat . . . . 14 g
  Saturated Fat . . . . . . 3 g
Cholesterol . . . . 72 mg
Sodium . . . . 735 mg
Carbohydrate . . . . . . 37 g
  Dietary Fiber . . . . 2 g
  Sugars . . . . 4 g
Protein . . . . 35 g

Curried Cornish Hens

Preparation Time: 20 minutes

Cornish game hens work great as an individual feast! Use the drumsticks and wings for appetizers the next day.

1 7–8 oz Rock Cornish game hen

1/2 cup cooked rice

1/2 tsp curry powder

1 Tbsp sliced pitted black olives

1 tsp chopped pimento

1 Tbsp mustard

1 tsp Worcestershire sauce

1 tsp honey

1/2 tsp sesame seeds

1. Preheat the oven to 350 degrees. Spray a small baking dish with nonstick cooking spray. Wash the hen thoroughly in clean water and remove the giblets (if present). Rinse thoroughly, blot dry with a paper towel, and place the hen in a small baking dish.

2. Mix together the rice, curry powder, olives, and pimento in a small bowl. Add a few drops of water if needed to mix well. Stuff the hen with the rice mixture. Whisk together the mustard, Worcestershire sauce, and honey in a separate bowl.

3. Baste the hen with the mustard sauce, using a small pastry brush or a spoon. Reserve the remaining liquid to baste throughout the cooking process. Sprinkle sesame seeds on top.

4. Bake for approximately 1 1/4 hours, or until the hen is lightly browned and the meat juices run clear when pricked with a fork.

Serves 2

Exchanges

1 Starch
2 Lean Meat
1 Fat

Calories 244
　Calories from Fat . . . 114
Total Fat . . . . 13 g
　Saturated Fat . . . . 3 g
Cholesterol . . . . 82 mg
Sodium . . . . 198 mg
Carbohydrate . . . . . . 16 g
　Dietary Fiber . . . . 0 g
　Sugars . . . . 4 g
Protein . . . . 16 g

Skinny Shepherd's Pie

Preparation Time: 15 minutes

Another variation of a casserole favorite for the microwave!

- 2 8-oz baking potatoes
- 1/4 cup nonfat milk, warmed
- 8 oz cooked ground turkey (97% fat-free)
- 1/2 cup chopped onion
- 1/2 cup frozen green beans
- 1/2 cup sliced carrots
- 1/2 cup low-sodium, condensed tomato soup
- 1/8 tsp black pepper
- 1/4 tsp thyme
- 1/4 tsp rosemary
- 1/4 tsp dried parsley
- 2 Tbsp grated low-fat cheddar cheese
- 1/4 tsp paprika

1. Pierce the potatoes and microwave in a microwave-safe dish for 7 minutes on high, or until tender. Cool slightly, then peel and mash with a fork in a small bowl. Add the warmed milk to the potatoes, blend, and set aside.

2. Mix together the turkey, onion, green beans, and carrots in a microwave- and oven-safe casserole dish. Cover and microwave for 5 minutes on high.

3. Set the oven to broil. Combine the soup, pepper, thyme, rosemary, and parsley. Pour the soup mixture over the meat and vegetables and microwave for 5 minutes on high.

4. Remove the dish from the microwave carefully. Spread the prepared mashed potatoes over the top with a large spoon and sprinkle with grated cheese and paprika. Broil under a conventional oven broiler until the cheese is hot and bubbly. Serve at once.

Serves 2

Exchanges

3 1/2 Starch
1 Vegetable
4 Very Lean Meat

Calories	448	
Calories from Fat	66	
Total Fat	7	g
Saturated Fat	2	g
Cholesterol	88	mg
Sodium	328	mg
Carbohydrate	55	g
Dietary Fiber	6	g
Sugars	13	g
Protein	41	g

Spicy Chicken Breasts

Preparation Time: 10 minutes

Cook one chicken breast half for a main dish, and save the other one for a tasty sandwich on a hoagie bun the next day!

1 boneless chicken breast, halved

1 tsp sesame oil

2 tsp Dijon mustard

1 Tbsp low-fat sour cream

2 Tbsp chopped onion

1/2 Tbsp chopped garlic

1/2 tsp paprika

Fresh ground pepper to taste

1. Preheat the oven to 375 degrees. Spray a small shallow baking dish with nonstick cooking spray and place the chicken in the baking dish.

2. Mix together the sesame oil, mustard, sour cream, onion, and garlic in a small bowl. Brush the sour cream mixture on both sides of each breast with a pastry brush.

3. Sprinkle the chicken with paprika and black pepper and bake for about 30 minutes.

4. To microwave, cover the baking dish loosely with plastic wrap. Microwave for 6–8 minutes on high, or until the juices run clear. Be sure to rotate the dish halfway through the cooking time for even cooking.

Serves 2

Exchanges

4 Very Lean Meat
1/2 Fat

Calories 172
  Calories from Fat . . . 50
Total Fat . . . . 6 g
  Saturated Fat . . . . . . 1 g
Cholesterol . . . . 72 mg
Sodium . . . . 141 mg
Carbohydrate . . . . 2 g
  Dietary Fiber . . . . 0 g
  Sugars . . . . 1 g
Protein . . . . 27 g

Tangy Apricot Chicken

Preparation Time: 3 minutes

Salad dressings can be the basis of many different sauces or dips, as in this delicious chicken.

2 chicken thighs, skin removed

1/4 cup fruit-sweetened apricot jam

2 Tbsp fat-free Thousand Island dressing

Fresh ground pepper to taste

1. Preheat the oven to 350 degrees. Spray a small baking dish with nonstick cooking spray. Wash the chicken and blot dry with paper towels.

2. Stir the jam into the dressing. Coat the chicken with the apricot mixture and place in the baking dish. Season with pepper to taste.

3. Bake for 20–25 minutes or until the meat juices run clear and the meat is cooked through.

Serves 1

Exchanges
2 Fruit
4 Lean Meat

Calories 333
  Calories from Fat . . . 98
Total Fat . . . . 11 g
  Saturated Fat . . . . . . 3 g
Cholesterol . . . . 99 mg
Sodium . . . . 366 mg
Carbohydrate . . . . . . 29 g
  Dietary Fiber . . . . 3 g
  Sugars . . . . 18 g
Protein . . . . 29 g

Tarragon Turkey Patty

Preparation Time: 10 minutes

A new twist for a simple entree!

- 1 tsp extra-virgin olive oil
- 1/4 lb ground turkey (97% fat-free)
- 2 Tbsp chopped onion
- 2 Tbsp dry bread crumbs
- 1 tsp dried parsley
- 1/4 tsp thyme
- 1/4 tsp tarragon
- Fresh ground pepper to taste
- 1 egg white
- 1 Tbsp flour

1. Mix together all ingredients except the flour in a small bowl. Form the turkey mixture into a 3/4-inch-thick patty. Heat the oil in a small skillet over medium heat.

2. Dredge the turkey patty in the flour and place in the skillet. Cook for about 5 minutes on each side, or until the juices run clear when pricked with a fork. Do not overcook.

Serves 1

Exchanges

1 1/2 Starch
4 Very Lean Meat
1 Monounsaturated Fat

Calories	302
Calories from Fat	89
Total Fat	10 g
Saturated Fat	2 g
Cholesterol	69 mg
Sodium	235 mg
Carbohydrate	18 g
Dietary Fiber	1 g
Sugars	2 g
Protein	33 g

Turkey Meat Loaf Mexicano

Preparation Time: 10 minutes

Serve this delicious meat loaf with Fast Spanish Rice (see recipe, p. 100) or No-Fried Mexican Beans (see recipe, p. 104).

4 oz ground turkey (97% fat-free)

1/8 cup crushed, fat-free, unsalted tortilla chips

1 Tbsp liquid egg substitute (may substitute 1 egg white)

2 dashes whole cumin seeds

2 Tbsp store-bought salsa

1 tsp chopped fresh cilantro

1. Preheat the oven to 350 degrees. Spray a small baking dish with nonstick cooking spray.

2. In a small bowl, combine all the ingredients and mix well.

3. Shape the meat mixture into a small loaf and place it in the center of the baking dish.

4. Bake for 20 minutes, or until the juices run clear when pricked with a fork.

Serves 1

Exchanges

1/2 Starch
4 Very Lean Meat

Calories 163
  Calories from Fat 9
Total Fat . . . . 1 g
  Saturated Fat . . . . . . 0 g
Cholesterol . . . . 75 mg
Sodium . . . . 178 mg
Carbohydrate . . . . 8 g
  Dietary Fiber . . . . 1 g
  Sugars . . . . 1 g
Protein . . . . 29 g

Beef & Pork

Basic Ground Beef

Preparation Time: 3 minutes

This mixture is used in a variety of different recipes. Divide the mixture into 4-oz portions and freeze in small freezer bags. Then thaw when you're ready to use!

1 1/2 lb lean ground chuck

1 Tbsp parsley flakes

1 tsp onion powder

1 tsp garlic powder

1/2 tsp black pepper

1/2 cup fine dry bread crumbs

1 Tbsp Worcestershire sauce

1. Thoroughly mix all the ingredients in a large bowl.

2. Divide the meat into six 4-oz portions and place in small freezer bags.

3. Freeze immediately. Use any refrigerated portions within 48 hours.

Serves 6

Exchanges

1/2 Starch
3 Lean Meat
1 Fat

Calories 255
  Calories from Fat . . . 129
Total Fat . . . . 16 g
  Saturated Fat . . . . . . 6 g
Cholesterol . . . . 71 mg
Sodium . . . . 161 mg
Carbohydrate . . . . 7 g
  Dietary Fiber . . . . 0 g
  Sugars . . . . 0 g
Protein . . . . 23 g

Deutsche Steak

Preparation Time: 15 minutes

This steak has a gourmet taste, but is so easy to make! Serve with fresh mashed potatoes and coleslaw.

1   5-oz top round steak

1/2   cup red wine vinegar

    Juice from 1 small lemon

2   tsp low-calorie margarine

1/2   cup sliced white mushrooms

1/4   cup sliced red onions

1/2   tsp paprika

    Fresh ground pepper to taste

1. Two days before serving, place the steak in a small shallow dish. Add the vinegar and lemon juice to the steak and cover it with plastic wrap. Marinate for 48 hours, turning twice each day.

2. When you are ready to cook, preheat the oven to 350 degrees and drain the marinade from the steak. Discard the marinade.

3. Heat the remaining ingredients in a heavy skillet over medium heat until the mixture is hot. Add the marinated steak and turn off the heat.

4. Place the skillet in the oven and cook for 30 minutes, or until the steak reaches desired doneness.

Serves 1

Exchanges

1   Starch
4   Lean Meat
1   Fat

Calories 259
  Calories from Fat 79
Total Fat . . . . 9 g
  Saturated Fat . . . . . . 1 g
Cholesterol . . . . 81 mg
Sodium . . . . 140 mg
Carbohydrate . . . . . . 11 g
  Dietary Fiber . . . . 2 g
  Sugars . . . . 6 g
Protein . . . . 34 g

Beefy Macaroni Casserole*

Preparation Time: 15 minutes

This home-style casserole tastes great with a crusty roll and salad.

1/2 cup uncooked, small macaroni

1 tsp extra-virgin olive oil

1 pkg Basic Ground Beef (thaw if necessary, or use 4 oz fresh ground chuck)

1 Tbsp chopped onion

3 Tbsp ketchup

1 tsp spicy brown mustard

1/8 tsp black pepper

1/4 tsp dried oregano

1/2 tsp dried parsley

1. Preheat the oven to 350 degrees. Spray a small oven-safe casserole dish with nonstick cooking spray.

2. Cook the macaroni without salt and drain well.

3. Heat the oil in a small skillet. Add the Basic Ground Beef and cook until browned. Drain off any excess fat. Add the chopped onion and continue to cook until onions are soft. Remove from the heat.

4. Combine the beef and onion mixture with the remaining ingredients and mix well. Spoon the mixture into the prepared casserole dish and bake for 20 minutes.

* This recipe is relatively high in sodium.

Serves 1

Exchanges

3 1/2 Starch
3 Lean Meat
1 Monounsaturated Fat

Calories 515
  Calories from Fat . . . 182
Total Fat . . . . 20 g
  Saturated Fat . . . . . . 6 g
Cholesterol . . . . 71 mg
Sodium . . . . 759 mg
Carbohydrate . . . . . . 53 g
  Dietary Fiber . . . . 3 g
  Sugars . . . . 8 g
Protein . . . . 29 g

New Shu Pork

Preparation Time: 15 minutes

This lighter version of mu shu pork is good with steamed rice and broccoli.

1/4	cup water
1/2	dried chili pepper
1	tsp peanut oil (or use canola oil)
1	3-oz boneless pork chop, thinly sliced
1/2	small onion, sliced
1	clove garlic, chopped
1	small zucchini, cut into 1/2-inch slices
1 1/2	cups shredded green cabbage
1	tsp lite soy sauce
1/8	tsp cayenne pepper
	Fresh ground pepper to taste

1. Heat the water in a small skillet over low heat. Add the dried chili pepper. Cook on medium-low heat for 15 minutes, or until the pepper softens. Remove the pepper to a small plate and allow it to cool. Save the water for later use.

2. When the pepper is cool to the touch, cut 1/2 inch off the top of the pepper along with the stem. If you prefer less "pepper heat," remove the seeds. Slice the remaining pepper in horizontal strips and set aside.

3. Heat the oil in a wok or medium nonstick skillet on medium-high heat. Add the pork strips and cook until the meat is no longer pink. Add

(continued)

Serves 1

Exchanges

1 Carbohydrate
(or 3 Vegetable)
3 Lean Meat
1/2 Fat

Calories 260
  Calories from Fat . . . 104
Total Fat . . . . 12 g
  Saturated Fat . . . . . . 3 g
Cholesterol . . . . 55 mg
Sodium . . . . 266 mg
Carbohydrate . . . . . . 17 g
  Dietary Fiber . . . . 6 g
  Sugars . . . . 10 g
Protein . . . . 23 g

New Shu Pork

(*continued*)

the onion, garlic, and zucchini, and stir-fry until the onion becomes transparent and soft. Reduce the heat to medium and add the shredded cabbage, stirring well.

4. Add the soy sauce, cayenne pepper, black pepper, chili pepper, and the reserved water. Cover and cook for 5–7 minutes, stirring every 2 minutes. Remove from the heat and serve.

Personal Pizza*

Preparation Time: 10 minutes

Don't want to order a whole pizza? Make your own!

1 6-inch pita bread

1 tsp extra-virgin olive oil

3 Tbsp low-sodium tomato sauce

1/2 tsp oregano

1/4 tsp thyme

1/4 tsp basil

1/4 tsp onion powder

1/4 tsp garlic powder

1/4 small onion, chopped

1/4 cup chopped fresh tomatoes

1 tsp grated Parmesan cheese

1 oz extra lean ham, sliced into strips

1. Preheat the oven to 425 degrees. Place the pita bread on a flat baking sheet. Drizzle the olive oil over the bread.

2. Combine the tomato sauce, oregano, thyme, basil, onion powder, and garlic powder in a small cup or bowl and mix well. Spread the sauce over the pita bread.

3. Place the ham strips on the pita bread like the spokes of a wheel. Sprinkle the onion on top of the ham. Place the chopped tomatoes around the edge of the pita bread.

4. Sprinkle Parmesan cheese on the pizza and bake for 10–12 minutes, until the crust is browned.

* This recipe is relatively high in sodium.

Serves 1

Exchanges

2 1/2 Starch
1 Vegetable
1 Lean Meat
1/2 Monounsaturated Fat

Calories 295
  Calories from Fat . . . 78
Total Fat . . . . 9 g
  Saturated Fat . . . . . . 2 g
Cholesterol . . . . 18 mg
Sodium . . . . 740 mg
Carbohydrate . . . . . . 42 g
  Dietary Fiber . . . . 3 g
  Sugars . . . . 6 g
Protein . . . . 13 g

Sauted Pork Strips

Preparation Time: 15 minutes

Use 2 small pork chops or a 4-oz lean pork loin for this dish.

1 tsp extra-virgin olive oil

2 Tbsp lite soy sauce

2 Tbsp white wine

1 tsp minced garlic

1/4 tsp rosemary

Fresh ground pepper to taste

4 oz lean boneless pork

1/4 cup thinly sliced onion

1/4 cup thinly sliced green or red bell peppers

1. Whisk together the olive oil, soy sauce, wine, garlic, rosemary, and black pepper in a small nonplastic bowl.

2. Cut the pork into strips approximately 1/4 inch thick and place them in the marinade. Cover and refrigerate for at least 8 hours, stirring once.

3. Spray a medium skillet with nonstick cooking spray. Drain the meat, discard the marinade, and place the strips in the skillet. Cook over medium-high heat for 1 minute, turning constantly, then add the sliced onion and bell pepper.

4. Reduce the heat to medium and cook for about 3 minutes. Season with additional pepper as desired. Continue cooking until the meat is cooked through and the onions and peppers are just tender, but still slightly crisp.

Serves 1

Exchanges

1 Vegetable
4 Lean Meat

Calories 240
  Calories from Fat . . . 96
Total Fat . . . . 11 g
  Saturated Fat . . . . . . 4 g
Cholesterol . . . . 78 mg
Sodium . . . . 466 mg
Carbohydrate . . . . 5 g
  Dietary Fiber . . . . 1 g
  Sugars . . . . 3 g
Protein . . . . 29 g

Steak with Citrus Mushroom Sauce

Preparation Time: 20 minutes

This is a nice meal for special occasions—use a small strip steak or tenderloin cut.

4 oz lean boneless steak

1 tsp extra-virgin olive oil

1/4 tsp black pepper

1/2 tsp onion powder

1 small orange

2 tsp low-calorie margarine

1/2 cup chopped mushrooms

1 Tbsp flour

1 bay leaf

Dash cayenne pepper

1 tsp chopped fresh cilantro

1. Set the oven to broil. Brush a thin layer of oil over the steak and sprinkle with black pepper and onion powder. Broil only until halfway done, about 3 minutes on each side. Remove the pan from the broiler.

2. Grate the orange to obtain 1 tsp of finely grated orange peel. Squeeze all the juice from the orange, straining to remove seeds and pulp. Set the juice aside.

3. Melt the margarine over medium heat in a small skillet. Add the chopped mushrooms and

(continued)

Serves 1

Exchanges

1/2 Starch
1   Fruit
4   Lean Meat
1/2 Monounsaturated Fat

Calories 343
  Calories from Fat . . . 130
Total Fat . . . . 14 g
  Saturated Fat . . . . . . 5 g
Cholesterol . . . . 75 mg
Sodium . . . . 119 mg
Carbohydrate . . . . . . 25 g
  Dietary Fiber . . . . 5 g
  Sugars . . . . 12 g
Protein . . . . 29 g

Steak with Citrus Mushroom Sauce

(continued)

cook for 6 minutes, stirring every 2 minutes. Add the flour. When the flour is browned, quickly add the orange juice, orange peel, bay leaf, and red pepper. Stir gently, reduce heat to low, cover, and let simmer for about 5 minutes, or until the sauce is slightly thickened.

4. Pour half the prepared sauce over the meat and return it to the broiler. Continue cooking until desired doneness. Place the meat on a serving plate and pour the remaining sauce over the meat. Top with freshly chopped cilantro and serve.

Stuffed Red Pepper

Preparation Time: 15 minutes

Try using different stuffing mixtures to change the taste of this dish. It's good with rye bread toast points and a fresh citrus salad.

1 pkg Basic Ground Beef (see p. 51; thaw if necessary, or use 4 oz ground chuck)

1/4 cup cooked brown rice

1 small tomato, peeled, seeded, and chopped

1 tsp Worcestershire sauce

1/4 tsp thyme

1/2 tsp instant minced onion

2 dashes hot pepper sauce

1 large red bell pepper

1/2 cup water

1 Tbsp shredded part-skim mozzarella cheese

1. Preheat the oven to 350 degrees. Brown the beef over medium heat in a small skillet. Drain the fat and continue cooking. Add the rice, tomato, Worcestershire sauce, dried thyme, and minced onion. Cook for 5 minutes, stirring frequently.

2. Add the hot pepper sauce to taste. Remove the skillet from the heat and set aside.

3. Remove 1 inch from the top of the red bell pepper, along with the white core and seeds. Rinse the pepper with water, drain, and place the pepper in the center of a small baking dish.

4. Spoon the meat and rice mixture into the cavity of the pepper. Add the water to the baking dish. Top the pepper with cheese and bake for 20–25 minutes, or until the pepper is slightly soft.

Serves 1

Exchanges

2 Starch
1 Vegetable
3 Lean Meat
1 Fat

Calories	395
Calories from Fat	145
Total Fat	16 g
Saturated Fat	6 g
Cholesterol	75 mg
Sodium	270 mg
Carbohydrate	34 g
Dietary Fiber	4 g
Sugars	7 g
Protein	28 g

Super Stuffed Spud

Preparation Time: 15 minutes

Use prepared sandwich meat slices for this quick meal.

1 10-oz baking potato

1 Tbsp low-fat sour cream

1/2 tsp parsley flakes

1/4 tsp onion powder

1/2 cup steamed broccoli florets

1/4 cup sauted small fresh mushrooms

1 oz extra lean ham, cooked and sliced

1. Bake the potato in the oven or microwave until done. Slice the potato lengthwise without going all the way through the skin.

2. Using a large tablespoon, carefully remove the potato flesh and place it in a small bowl. Place the empty potato skin on a serving plate. Add the sour cream, parsley flakes, and onion powder to the potato flesh and mix well.

3. Spoon the mixture back into the potato jacket. Add the broccoli, mushrooms, and ham. Serve immediately.

4. Other topping ideas include onions, peppers, tomatoes, shredded low-fat cheese, chopped egg, fresh spinach, black beans, and leftover shredded meat.

Serves 1

Exchanges

4 Starch
1 Very Lean Meat

Calories 340
  Calories from Fat . . . 29
Total Fat . . . . 3 g
  Saturated Fat . . . . . . 1 g
Cholesterol . . . . 15 mg
Sodium . . . . 431 mg
Carbohydrate . . . . . 66 g
  Dietary Fiber . . . . 9 g
  Sugars . . . . 7 g
Protein . . . . 15 g

Tacos Supreme

Preparation Time: 15 minutes

Serve these tasty tacos with No-Fried Mexican Beans (see recipe, p. 104) and baked tortilla chips for a festive meal.

1 pkg Basic Ground Beef (see p. 51; thaw if necessary, or use 4 oz ground chuck)

1 Tbsp chopped onions

1/4 tsp ground cumin

1 Tbsp prepared salsa

2 6-inch flour tortillas

2 Tbsp chopped tomatoes

2 pieces lettuce, shredded

1. Brown the beef with the onions in a small skillet over medium heat until the onions are softened. Drain off the fat.

2. Add the cumin and salsa and cook for 2 minutes. Heat the tortillas for 1 minute per side over medium heat in a nonstick skillet. Use half of the mixture to stuff each tortilla.

3. Add the tomato and lettuce to each tortilla. Top with additional salsa to taste.

Serves 1

Exchanges

3 Starch
3 Lean Meat
1 1/2 Fat

Calories 480
  Calories from Fat . . . 173
Total Fat . . . . 19 g
  Saturated Fat . . . . . . 6 g
Cholesterol . . . . 71 mg
Sodium . . . . 512 mg
Carbohydrate . . . . . . 46 g
  Dietary Fiber . . . . 4 g
  Sugars . . . . 4 g
Protein . . . . 29 g

Vietnamese Pork

Preparation Time: 10 minutes

This dish is served at our favorite Vietnamese restaurant. You can use any leftover meat for this recipe to make a fresh new entree!

1 cup green leaf lettuce

1 cup cooked rice

1/2 small cucumber, peeled and sliced

1 Tbsp chopped fresh cilantro

1 Tbsp chopped fresh mint leaves

3 oz lean pork, cooked and sliced

1 Tbsp chopped dry-roasted peanuts

1 tsp lite soy sauce

2 Tbsp Nuom Chuc Sauce (see recipe, p. 64)

1. Chop the lettuce into long strips and place in a small, deep bowl. In layers, add the rice and cucumber. Sprinkle with the cilantro and mint.

2. Add the cooked pork, peanuts, and soy sauce. Add the Nuom Chuc sauce to taste and serve.

Serves 1

Exchanges

4 Starch
3 Very Lean Meat
1/2 Fat

Calories	449
Calories from Fat	83
Total Fat	9 g
Saturated Fat	2 g
Cholesterol	68 mg
Sodium	645 mg
Carbohydrate	57 g
Dietary Fiber	3 g
Sugars	9 g
Protein	33 g

Nuom Chuc Sauce

Preparation Time: 5 minutes

Prepare this sauce 2 hours before serving for the best flavor. The leftover sauce will stay stored in the refrigerator in a covered glass container for 1 week.

1 Tbsp rice wine vinegar

1 Tbsp fresh lime juice

2 Tbsp prepared fish sauce

2 Tbsp water

1 tsp dry white wine

1 Tbsp sugar

1 clove garlic, minced

1/4 tsp cayenne pepper

1 Tbsp finely julienned carrot

1 Tbsp finely julienned green onion

Combine all the ingredients in a small, nonplastic bowl and stir until the sugar dissolves.

Serves 4

Serving size: 2 Tbsp

Exchanges

1/2 Carbohydrate

Calories 24
  Calories from Fat 0
Total Fat . . . . .0 g
  Saturated Fat . . . . . .0 g
Cholesterol . . . . .0 mg
Sodium . . . . .316 mg
Carbohydrate . . . . . . .6 g
  Dietary Fiber . . . . . . .0 g
  Sugars . . . . .5 g
Protein . . . . .1 g

Savory Seafood

Baked Pepper Fish

Preparation Time: 15 minutes

A low-fat way to prepare a fish filet!

1　4-oz fish filet (use a firm fish, such as halibut or swordfish)

2　Tbsp fat-free Ranch dressing

　　Dash cayenne pepper

1/2　large red bell pepper, thinly sliced

1　small onion, peeled and thinly sliced

1/2　cup broccoli florets, washed and drained

1. Preheat the oven to 450 degrees. Spray a 12-inch square of heavy aluminum foil with nonstick cooking spray.

2. Place the filet on the foil. Spread the dressing over the filet with a small spoon or pastry brush and sprinkle with red pepper. Arrange the vegetables over the fish.

3. Fold the foil over and seal the edges well. Place the foil packet in the middle of the oven,

(continued)

Serves 1

Exchanges

1　Carbohydrate
2　Vegetable
2　Very Lean Meat

Calories 198
　Calories from Fat . . . 10
Total Fat . . . . 1 g
　Saturated Fat . . . . 0 g
Cholesterol . . . . 49 mg
Sodium . . . . 384 mg
Carbohydrate . . . . 24 g
　Dietary Fiber . . . . 3 g
　Sugars . . . . 8 g
Protein . . . . 24 g

Baked Pepper Fish

(*continued*)

directly on the rack. To prevent spills, you may want to place the foil packet on a small baking sheet.

4. Bake for 20 minutes, or until the fish is white through the center and flakes easily with a fork.

5. To microwave, place the filet and other ingredients directly on a microwave-safe plate (you can omit the nonstick cooking spray). Cover with plastic wrap and microwave on high for 5 minutes or until done. Remember to turn the plate halfway through the cooking time for even cooking.

Buttery Linguine with Shrimp

Preparation Time: 20 minutes

Love buttery-flavored pastas? Try this variation for fewer calories. Serve with a spinach salad and garlic bread.

1 tsp extra-virgin olive oil

6 medium shrimp, peeled, tails removed, rinsed, and drained

6 mushrooms, sliced

1 clove garlic

1 cup cooked fettucine or linguine

1 1/2-oz envelope Artificial Butter Flavor Mix

1 tsp Italian seasoning

1 Tbsp chopped fresh basil leaves

Fresh ground pepper to taste

1. Heat the oil in a medium skillet over medium heat. Add the shrimp and cook until the shrimp is pink and white.

2. Add the mushrooms and garlic, reduce heat to low, and cook for 3 minutes. Add the pasta to the skillet and toss well.

3. Prepare the butter flavor mix according to directions in a small measuring cup. Add 2 Tbsp of liquefied butter mix to the skillet and stir well.

4. Add the seasoning, basil, and black pepper. Continue to cook over low heat until the linguine is well heated.

Serves 1

Exchanges

3 1/2 Starch
1 Lean Meat

Calories	333
Calories from Fat	59
Total Fat	7 g
Saturated Fat	1 g
Cholesterol	116 mg
Sodium	287 mg
Carbohydrate	53 g
Dietary Fiber	4 g
Sugars	8 g
Protein	21 g

Crab Toast*

Preparation Time: 20 minutes

Serve this with fresh fruit or melon for brunch, lunch, or a light supper.

- 1/4 cup shredded imitation crab meat
- 1/2 cup liquid egg substitute
- 1/4 tsp tarragon
- 2 dashes paprika
- 1 Tbsp low-calorie margarine
- 2 slices whole-grain bread (use thickly sliced bread)
- 1 small tomato, thinly sliced

1. Preheat a griddle or a large skillet to medium heat. In a small bowl, combine the shredded crab, egg substitute, tarragon, and paprika. Mix well.

2. Spread the margarine on both sides of the bread slices. Using a biscuit cutter, cut out a large circle in each slice of bread. Save these centers.

3. Place the bread slices (not the centers!) on the hot griddle. Carefully spoon the crab/egg mixture into the holes in the center of each slice until they are almost full. (You may have a few small spoonfuls of batter left over—this can be

(continued)

Serves 1

Exchanges
2 Starch
1 Vegetable
2 Lean Meat

Calories 318
  Calories from Fat 71
Total Fat . . . . 8 g
  Saturated Fat . . . . 1 g
Cholesterol . . . . 14 mg
Sodium . . . . 932 mg
Carbohydrate . . . . 39 g
  Dietary Fiber . . . . 5 g
  Sugars . . . . 12 g
Protein . . . . 24 g

Crab Toast

(*continued*)

cooked separately.) Cook each bread slice, turning once, until it is golden brown and the center is solid. Place both pieces on a serving plate.

4. Grill the bread circles on both sides. Place a tomato slice on each grilled circle of bread and add the circles to the serving plate. Serve at once.

* This recipe is high in sodium!

Louisiana Light Creole Sauce

Preparation Time: 5 minutes

Pour this sauce over fish or shrimp and bake! This sauce goes well with rice, pasta, or couscous.

1/2 cup chopped, drained tomatoes

1 stalk celery, chopped

2 Tbsp chopped green bell pepper

2 Tbsp chopped onion

1 clove garlic, chopped

2 dashes cayenne pepper

Fresh ground pepper to taste

1 tsp extra-virgin olive oil

Combine all ingredients in a small bowl. Pour over chicken or seafood and bake, or heat and serve on the side.

Serves 1

Exchanges

2 Vegetable
1 Monounsaturated Fat

Calories 88
  Calories from Fat . . . 45
Total Fat . . . . 5 g
  Saturated Fat . . . . 1 g
Cholesterol . . . . 0 mg
Sodium . . . . 249 mg
Carbohydrate . . . . . . 11 g
  Dietary Fiber . . . . 3 g
  Sugars . . . . 6 g
Protein . . . . 2 g

Mermaid Filet

Preparation Time: 15 minutes

Like the taste of mild-flavored fish? Try this cooking technique. Serve with steamed rice or cornbread.

1 tsp low-calorie margarine, softened

1 4-oz cod filet

1 Tbsp nonfat milk

2 dashes paprika

2 pinches parsley

Dash lemon pepper

1. Preheat the oven to 400 degrees. Cut a 12-inch square of heavy-duty aluminum foil or baking parchment paper. Place the square on a baking sheet and spread the margarine in the center with a pastry brush or small spoon in the approximate size of the filet.

2. Place the filet on top of the margarine layer. Gently pull the sides of the square up to form a sealable pouch, but do not yet seal.

3. Carefully spoon the milk over the filet. Add the paprika, parsley, and lemon pepper and seal the pouch with the seam over the top of the filet.

4. Cook for 10–12 minutes. Use kitchen shears or a small knife to open the foil pouch. Use caution when cutting open the pouch, because steam will escape. Fish flesh should be white and firm and should flake easily with a fork.

Serves 1

Exchanges

3 Very Lean Meat

Calories	114
Calories from Fat	24
Total Fat	3 g
Saturated Fat	0 g
Cholesterol	49 mg
Sodium	98 mg
Carbohydrate	1 g
Dietary Fiber	0 g
Sugars	1 g
Protein	21 g

Moroccan Tuna with Herb Salsa

Preparation Time: 15 minutes

If you can't get fresh tuna steaks, substitute drained, canned tuna and serve this recipe as a cold dish.

1   5-oz tuna steak

1/2   tsp extra-virgin olive oil

1   small lemon, peeled, seeded, pith removed, and chopped

1   small lime, peeled, seeded, pith removed, and chopped

1   Tbsp chopped green onions

1   Tbsp chopped fresh cilantro

1   Tbsp chopped fresh parsley

3   Tbsp unsweetened orange juice

1/8   tsp salt

1   tsp extra-virgin olive oil

2   tsp sugar

1. Set the oven to broil. Lightly coat the tuna steak with the olive oil and broil for about 3–5 minutes on each side, until the flesh is cooked through and flakes easily with a fork.

2. Combine the remaining ingredients, pour the salsa over the tuna steak, and serve.

3. The extra salsa may be stored for 2–3 days, covered, in the refrigerator. It tastes great on broiled or baked chicken, too!

Serves 1

Exchanges

2   Carbohydrate
4   Lean Meat

Calories 347
  Calories from Fat . . 123
Total Fat . . . . 14 g
  Saturated Fat . . . . 3 g
Cholesterol . . . . 52 mg
Sodium . . . . 339 mg
Carbohydrate . . . . 28 g
  Dietary Fiber . . . . 5 g
  Sugars . . . . 11 g
Protein . . . . 33 g

Southwestern Filet

Preparation Time: 10 minutes

This is an easy way to flavor fish. Try black beans and rice with this meal!

1 4-oz filet tuna, swordfish, or any firm fish

1 tsp corn oil

1 Tbsp stone-ground yellow cornmeal

1/2 small lime

1/2 small onion, thinly sliced

Dash cayenne pepper

2 Tbsp store-bought salsa

1. Preheat the oven to 400 degrees. Coat both sides of the filet with the oil and dredge in the cornmeal.

2. Place the filet on a broiler pan. Squeeze the lime onto the filet. Add the onions and sprinkle the pepper on top.

3. Bake for 15 minutes or until the flesh is white and flaky. Serve with salsa.

Serves 1

Exchanges

1 Starch
1 Vegetable
3 Lean Meat

Calories 264
  Calories from Fat . . . 89
Total Fat . . . . 10 g
  Saturated Fat . . . . 2 g
Cholesterol . . . . 44 mg
Sodium . . . . 185 mg
Carbohydrate . . . . 19 g
  Dietary Fiber . . . . 2 g
  Sugars . . . . 7 g
Protein . . . . 25 g

Tangy Fish Kabobs

Preparation Time: 20 minutes

This is an easy-to-fix main course using a different cooking technique for fish and vegetables. Get fresh vegetable items off the grocery store salad bar to prevent waste!

8 oz fresh fish filets (if using frozen, thaw and drain)

1 Tbsp extra-virgin olive oil

1 Tbsp lemon juice

2 tsp fresh basil

2 tsp fresh oregano

2 tsp fresh thyme

1 tsp dried rosemary

6 mushrooms

1 small zucchini, cut into 1/2-inch slices

1 small onion, cut into small wedges

1 medium red or green bell pepper, cut into 1-inch chunks

4 cherry tomatoes

1 small yellow squash, cut in 1/2-inch slices

3 tsp lite soy sauce

1. Cut filets into 1 1/2-inch pieces and place in a small bowl. Whisk together the oil, lemon juice, basil, oregano, thyme, and rosemary and pour over the fish, tossing gently to coat. Cover tightly and marinate in the refrigerator for 2 hours.

2. Preheat the oven to 400 degrees. Remove the fish from the marinade and discard the marinade. Combine all the vegetables and steam lightly for about 3 minutes.

3. Assemble the kabobs on 4 skewers, alternating fish and vegetable pieces as desired. Spray the rack on a broiler pan with nonstick cooking spray and place the skewers on the rack.

4. Bake for 6 minutes. Turn the kabobs and bake for 6–7 minutes more or until the fish flakes easily with a fork.

Serves 2

Exchanges

1 Carbohydrate
4 Very Lean Meat

Calories 212
  Calories from Fat . . . 39
Total Fat . . . . 4 g
  Saturated Fat . . . . 1 g
Cholesterol . . . . 41 mg
Sodium . . . . 364 mg
Carbohydrate . . . . 18 g
  Dietary Fiber . . . . 4 g
  Sugars . . . . 9 g
Protein . . . . 26 g

Meatless Meals

Benedictine Sandwich

Preparation Time: 10 minutes

This Southern favorite is good with sliced tomatoes and a bowl of soup.

1 6-oz cucumber, peeled and halved horizontally

2 Tbsp reduced-fat cream cheese

2 tsp lite mayonnaise

1/4 tsp instant minced onion

1/4 tsp lemon juice

Dash hot pepper sauce

1–2 drops green food coloring

2 slices whole-grain bread, toasted

1. Remove any large seeds from the cucumber with a spoon and grate the flesh with a standard grater into a small bowl.

2. Add the remaining ingredients except the bread and mix until fairly smooth and easy to spread. Refrigerate the filling for 1 hour.

3. Spread the mixture on the toasted whole-grain bread. Cut into quarters diagonally and serve.

Serves 1

Exchanges

2 Starch
1 Vegetable
1 Saturated Fat

Calories 234
 Calories from Fat . . . 67
Total Fat . . . . 7 g
 Saturated Fat . . . . . . 4 g
Cholesterol . . . . 15 mg
Sodium . . . . 519 mg
Carbohydrate . . . . . . 33 g
 Dietary Fiber . . . . . . 5 g
 Sugars . . . . 8 g
Protein . . . . 10 g

Broiled Vegetable Sandwich*

Preparation Time: 15 minutes

This is a hearty sandwich, full of vitamins. Use the remaining vegetable ingredients to make a salad for the next day.

  1 small zucchini, julienned

1/2 cup cider vinegar

  1 tsp chopped, pickled jalapeno peppers

1/2 medium red bell pepper, julienned

  1 slice tomato

  1 slice sweet red onion

  2 tsp extra-virgin olive oil

  3 dashes black pepper

  1 3 1/2-oz deli-style rye roll

  1 slice low-fat Swiss cheese

1. Place the zucchini strips in a small container with a lid and add the cider vinegar and jalapeno peppers. Cover and refrigerate for at least 2 hours.

2. Set the oven to broil and spray the broiler pan with nonstick cooking spray. Drain the marinade from the zucchini and place the strips on the broiler pan.

3. Add the bell pepper, tomato, and onion to the broiler pan. Drizzle with olive oil and sprinkle with black pepper.

4. Broil until the vegetables are brown and soft, about 15 minutes. Using a pair of tongs, carefully layer the vegetables on a roll and top with cheese. For more flavor, marinate all the vegetables for 8 hours before broiling.

* This recipe is high in sodium.

Serves 1

Exchanges

4 Starch
1 Lean Meat

Calories 366
  Calories from Fat . . . 63
Total Fat . . . . 7 g
  Saturated Fat . . . . . . 3 g
Cholesterol . . . . 10 mg
Sodium . . . . 759 mg
Carbohydrate . . . . . . 59 g
  Dietary Fiber . . . . 8 g
  Sugars . . . . 10 g
Protein . . . . 19 g

Four-Pepper Pasta

Preparation Time: 20 minutes

Use different varieties of pasta to change the look of this dish!

1/2 medium red bell pepper, cut into 1-inch chunks

1/2 medium green bell pepper, cut into 1-inch chunks

1/4 cup sliced red onion

1 tsp extra-virgin olive oil

1/2 tsp chopped garlic

1 tsp chopped jalapeno peppers

1/8 tsp cayenne pepper

Dash salt

1 cup cooked pasta (try spinach or whole-wheat)

1. Set the oven to broil. Place the red and green bell peppers and the red onions in a small bowl. Add the oil and toss until each piece is lightly coated with the oil.

2. Arrange the peppers and onion on the broiler pan. Broil until thoroughly roasted. (Some people like their roasted vegetables slightly singed with black!)

3. Spray a medium skillet with nonstick cooking spray and heat over medium-high heat. Add the garlic and jalapeno peppers, stirring quickly. Add the broiled peppers and onions. Sprinkle cayenne pepper and salt over the vegetables and heat thoroughly, about 2 minutes.

4. Add the cooked pasta to the skillet and toss with the vegetables until well mixed.

Serves 1

Exchanges

3 Starch
1 Vegetable
1/2 Monounsaturated Fat

Calories 283
  Calories from Fat . . . 51
Total Fat . . . . 6 g
  Saturated Fat . . . . . . 1 g
Cholesterol . . . . 0 mg
Sodium . . . . 149 mg
Carbohydrate . . . . . 54 g
  Dietary Fiber . . . . 9 g
  Sugars . . . . 9 g
Protein . . . . 10 g

Hoppin' Jane

Preparation Time: 20 minutes

This variation on Hoppin' John is great served with cornbread.

1 tsp extra-virgin olive oil

2 Tbsp chopped red onion

1/4 cup cooked black-eyed peas

1 tsp black pepper

1/2 cup cooked brown rice

2 Tbsp chopped tomato

1 hard-boiled egg white, chopped

1 tsp chopped fresh parsley

Dash hot pepper sauce

1. Heat the oil in a small skillet on medium-high heat. Add the red onion and cook until soft, stirring often.

2. Add the black-eyed peas and pepper, stirring continuously until thoroughly heated.

3. Spread the warmed brown rice on a serving plate and top with the hot skillet mixture.

4. Sprinkle the mixture with the tomato, egg white, and parsley. Season as desired with hot pepper sauce and serve.

Serves 1

Exchanges

2 1/2 Starch
1/2 Monounsaturated Fat

Calories 231
  Calories from Fat . . . 52
Total Fat . . . . 6 g
  Saturated Fat . . . . 1 g
Cholesterol . . . . 0 mg
Sodium . . . . 65 mg
Carbohydrate . . . . 35 g
  Dietary Fiber . . . . 5 g
  Sugars . . . . 5 g
Protein . . . . 10 g

Individual Cheese and Tomato Quiche*

Preparation Time: 10 minutes

You can add your own favorite quiche ingredients to this basic recipe.

1/2 cup liquid egg substitute

1 cup nonfat milk

1 Tbsp regular nonfat dry milk

1 tsp black pepper

1/2 cup grated low-fat cheddar cheese

1/4 cup chopped sun-dried tomatoes (not packed in oil, or use 1/3 cup fresh diced tomatoes)

1 tsp basil

Dash paprika

1. Preheat the oven to 350 degrees. Spray a 6-inch pie pan with nonstick cooking spray or spray 3 muffin compartments of a muffin tin (add water to the unused cups before placing in the oven).

2. Combine all the ingredients in a small bowl. The batter will be chunky. Pour the batter into the prepared pan and sprinkle with additional paprika if desired.

3. Bake for 30 minutes or until a knife inserted into the center draws out clean. Let the quiche stand 5 minutes before serving.

* *This recipe is very high in sodium!*

Serves 1

Exchanges

1 Skim Milk
1/2 Carbohydrate
1 Vegetable
4 Very Lean Meat

Calories 304
 Calories from Fat . . . 44
Total Fat . . . . 5 g
 Saturated Fat . . . . 3 g
Cholesterol . . . . 17 mg
Sodium . . . . 1000 mg
Carbohydrate . . . . 26 g
 Dietary Fiber . . . . 2 g
 Sugars . . . . 17 g
Protein . . . . 39 g

Rice and Black Bean Mediterranean Delight

Preparation Time: 15 minutes

This hearty main dish is good served with a crisp salad and warm whole-wheat rolls.

1   cup red leaf lettuce, washed and torn

3/4   cup cooked long-grain rice

1/2   small cucumber, peeled and sliced

4   oz canned black beans, drained and rinsed

1/2   tsp ground cumin

2   dashes hot pepper sauce (or 1/2 tsp juice from pickled jalapeno peppers)

Fresh ground pepper to taste

3   cherry tomatoes, chopped

2   Tbsp chopped green onions

1   Tbsp chopped fresh cilantro

1   small lemon, halved

1   Tbsp balsamic vinegar

1   Tbsp part-skim feta cheese

1. Arrange the lettuce to cover a dinner plate. Spoon the cooked rice over the lettuce to form a circle. Cut the cucumber slices in half and arrange them around the rice circle.

2. Combine the beans, cumin, hot sauce, and pepper in a small microwave-safe bowl. Cover and cook on medium for 60–90 seconds, or until the beans are hot.

3. Pour the bean mixture over the rice. Top with the tomatoes, green onions, and cilantro.

4. Squeeze half of the lemon over the entire plate. Slice the remaining lemon into half-circles and place them between the cucumber halves. Sprinkle with balsamic vinegar and top with feta cheese to serve.

Serves 1

Exchanges

4 1/2 Starch
1 Vegetable
1 Lean Meat

Calories 436
  Calories from Fat . . . 66
Total Fat . . . . 7 g
  Saturated Fat . . . . 5 g
Cholesterol . . . . 20 mg
Sodium . . . . 546 mg
Carbohydrate . . . . 73 g
  Dietary Fiber . . . . . . 13 g
  Sugars . . . . 10 g
Protein . . . . 21 g

Steve's Spinach Pesto with Angel Hair Pasta

Preparation Time: 15 minutes

Popeye would approve of this vitamin-packed dish!

- 1 cup fresh spinach, stems removed, washed and torn
- 2 Tbsp hot low-fat, low-sodium chicken broth
- 1 Tbsp extra-virgin olive oil
- 2 tsp lemon juice
- 1 Tbsp toasted pine nuts
- 1 Tbsp grated Parmesan cheese
- 1 tsp minced garlic
- 1/2 tsp dried basil
- 1/2 tsp red wine or balsamic vinegar
- 2 dashes black pepper
- 1 cup cooked angel hair pasta

1. Combine all the ingredients except the pasta in a food processor or blender. Do not over-blend.

2. Pour the mixture into a medium skillet and cook over medium heat for about 3 minutes. The sauce should be thoroughly heated.

3. Add the pasta and toss to coat. Cook for about 3 minutes, or until the pasta is hot. Serve immediately.

Serves 1

Exchanges

3 Starch
3 1/2 Monounsaturated Fat

Calories	386
Calories from Fat	197
Total Fat	22 g
Saturated Fat	4 g
Cholesterol	8 mg
Sodium	174 mg
Carbohydrate	42 g
Dietary Fiber	4 g
Sugars	3 g
Protein	13 g

Tofu Salad Sandwich

Preparation Time: 8 minutes

This version is much lower in cholesterol and fat than traditional egg salad, yet still tastes great! It's good served on toasted whole-grain bread, half a bagel, crackers, or an English muffin.

2 oz firm tofu

1/2 tsp spicy brown mustard

1 Tbsp low-fat plain yogurt

1 tsp lite mayonnaise

2 tsp sweet pickle relish

Fresh ground pepper to taste

1 tsp chopped pimento

Place the tofu in a small bowl and mash it into fine crumbs with a fork. Add the remaining ingredients and mix well.

Serves 1

Exchanges

1/2 Carbohydrate
1 Very Lean Meat

Calories 71
  Calories from Fat . . . 26
Total Fat . . . . 3 g
  Saturated Fat . . . . 0 g
Cholesterol . . . . 0 mg
Sodium . . . . 175 mg
Carbohydrate . . . . 6 g
  Dietary Fiber . . . . 1 g
  Sugars . . . . 5 g
Protein . . . . 6 g

Wall of China Stir-Fry

Preparation Time: 20 minutes

Stir-frying really preserves the nutrient content of vegetables. Since each addition to the wok reduces the cooking temperature, adding ingredients in stages helps to stabilize the heat and allows you to achieve true stir-frying.

1 1/2　tsp lite soy sauce

1 1/2　tsp dry sherry

1/4　tsp sesame oil

1　clove garlic, minced

5　drops hot pepper sauce

4　oz firm tofu, cut into small cubes

1/2　tsp canola oil (or try peanut oil for more authentic flavor)

1/4　cup diced celery

1/2　cup fresh broccoli

1/4　cup sliced onion

1/4　cup chopped green bell pepper

2/3　cup cooked brown rice

1. Combine the soy sauce, sherry, sesame oil, garlic, and hot pepper sauce in a small bowl or container with a lid. Gently stir in the tofu. Cover and refrigerate for at least 4 hours (overnight is best).

2. Spray a skillet with nonstick cooking spray, or use a seasoned wok, and heat over medium-high heat. Add the oil, celery, and broccoli and cook for 3–4 minutes, stirring constantly with a wooden paddle or nonstick spatula.

3. Add the onion and bell pepper and continue stir-frying for 5 minutes. Add the tofu with the soy marinade to the vegetables. Cook, stirring constantly, for about 3–5 minutes or until the tofu is heated through.

4. Serve immediately over the brown rice.

Serves 1

Exchanges
3　Starch
1　Medium-Fat Meat
1/2　Fat

Calories 333
　Calories from Fat . . . 96
Total Fat . . . . 11 g
　Saturated Fat . . . . 1 g
Cholesterol . . . . 0 mg
Sodium . . . . 366 mg
Carbohydrate . . . . . . 46 g
　Dietary Fiber . . . . 8 g
　Sugars . . . . 8 g
Protein . . . . 17 g

Side
Dishes

Acorn Squash with Apples

Preparation Time: 30 minutes

This is a great side dish for cool fall days.

1 acorn squash, halved lengthwise, strings and seeds removed

1 tsp brown sugar

1 tsp low-calorie margarine

2 tsp chopped walnuts

1/4 cup unpeeled, chopped, tart apples

1/8 tsp nutmeg

1 cup water

1. Preheat the oven to 350 degrees. Place half of the squash in a small glass or ceramic baking dish and sprinkle with brown sugar.

2. Mix together the margarine, walnuts, apples, and nutmeg thoroughly and spoon the mixture into the squash cavity.

3. Place the remaining squash half in the baking dish, but do not stuff. Add 1 cup of water to the dish.

4. Bake for about 30 minutes or until the squash is soft when pricked with a fork all the way through. Serve the stuffed acorn squash immediately. When the unstuffed squash has cooled, wrap it in plastic wrap for use in Acorn Squash Souffle (see recipe, p. 92).

Serves 1

Exchanges

2 Starch

Calories 156
  Calories from Fat . . . 58
Total Fat . . . . 6 g
  Saturated Fat . . . . . . 2 g
Cholesterol . . . . 0 mg
Sodium . . . . 52 mg
Carbohydrate . . . . . . 26 g
  Dietary Fiber . . . . . . 6 g
  Sugars . . . . 14 g
Protein . . . . 2 g

Acorn Squash Souffle

Preparation Time: 15 minutes

Serve this souffle with fresh steamed green beans and a whole-wheat roll.

1/2 cooked acorn squash

1/2 cup prepared and cooled instant mashed potatoes

1 beaten egg

Fresh ground pepper to taste

Dash salt

1 tsp low-calorie margarine

1. Preheat the oven to 375 degrees. Scoop the pulp from the squash into a small bowl.

2. Add the mashed potatoes, egg, pepper, and salt and blend well. Spoon the mixture into a small casserole dish.

3. Bake for 20 minutes or until slightly puffed and lightly browned. Add margarine to taste.

Serves 1

Exchanges
2 Starch
1 Medium-Fat Meat
1/2 Fat

Calories 256
  Calories from Fat . . 100
Total Fat . . . . 11 g
  Saturated Fat . . . . . . 5 g
Cholesterol . . . . 227 mg
Sodium . . . . 557 mg
Carbohydrate . . . . . . 33 g
  Dietary Fiber . . . . 7 g
  Sugars . . . . 8 g
Protein . . . . 9 g

Bill's Tomatoes with Dill

Preparation Time: 5 minutes

This is an easy summer side dish.

1 large tomato

1 tsp lite mayonnaise

1 tsp Parmesan cheese

1/4 tsp dill

1/2 tsp oregano

1/4 tsp basil

Dash cayenne pepper

Fresh ground pepper to taste

1. Set the oven on broil. Slice 1/2 to 1 inch off the top of the tomato so that a large flat surface of tomato flesh is exposed. (If you can't get the tomato to sit up by itself, wrap some foil around the base of the tomato to anchor it.)

2. Spread the mayonnaise on top of the tomato. Top with the Parmesan cheese and sprinkle with the spices. Broil for 3–5 minutes or until the tomato is hot and the topping is bubbly.

Serves 1

Exchanges

2 Vegetable

Calories 56
  Calories from Fat . . . 15
Total Fat . . . . 2 g
  Saturated Fat . . . . . . 1 g
Cholesterol . . . . 3 mg
Sodium . . . . 105 mg
Carbohydrate . . . . . . 10 g
  Dietary Fiber . . . . 2 g
  Sugars . . . . 6 g
Protein . . . . 3 g

Bravo Green Beans

Preparation Time: 5 minutes

Use the single-serving canned vegetables to avoid leftovers.

1/2 cup canned green beans, drained

2 Tbsp chopped onion

1 plum tomato, diced

2 Tbsp low-fat sour cream

1 Tbsp fat-free Italian dressing

Combine all ingredients. Refrigerate before serving.

Serves 1

Exchanges

1 Carbohydrate

Calories 74
  Calories from Fat 4
Total Fat . . . . 0 g
  Saturated Fat . . . . . . 0 g
Cholesterol . . . . 0 mg
Sodium . . . . 394 mg
Carbohydrate . . . . . . 14 g
  Dietary Fiber . . . . 3 g
  Sugars . . . . 9 g
Protein . . . . 4 g

Cider Sweet Potatoes

Preparation Time: 10 minutes

Use canned sweet potatoes for this quick recipe.

1/4	cup unsweetened apple juice
1 1/2	tsp low-calorie margarine
2	tsp brown sugar
1/2	large, tart apple, diced
1/3	tsp nutmeg
1	8-oz can sweet potatoes, drained

1. Preheat the oven to 350 degrees. Combine all the ingredients except the sweet potatoes in a small saucepan over medium heat. Stir until all of the sugar is dissolved and the margarine is melted.

2. Spray a small casserole dish with nonstick cooking spray. Place the sweet potatoes in the dish. Carefully pour the hot apple mixture over the sweet potatoes. Bake for 25 minutes.

Serves 2

Exchanges

1 1/2 Starch
1 Fruit
1/2 Fat

Calories 191
　Calories from Fat . . . 30
Total Fat . . . . 3 g
　Saturated Fat . . . . 1 g
Cholesterol . . . . 0 mg
Sodium . . . . 95 mg
Carbohydrate . . . . . . 40 g
　Dietary Fiber . . . . 5 g
　Sugars . . . . 32 g
Protein . . . . 2 g

Corn Pudding

Preparation Time: 15 minutes

Everyone likes corn pudding! Add your favorite extra ingredients to this basic recipe (try pimento, cornmeal, or chopped onion).

1/2 cup corn (thawed or frozen), rinsed and drained

1 beaten egg white

1/4 cup nonfat milk

1 1/2 tsp melted low-calorie margarine

1 Tbsp flour

2 tsp sugar

1/8 tsp paprika

Fresh ground pepper to taste

1. Preheat the oven to 375 degrees. Coat a medium ramekin baking dish or small casserole dish with nonstick cooking spray. (You can also use 2 muffin compartments of a muffin tin, but fill the remaining compartments with water before baking.)

2. Combine all the ingredients in a small bowl and pour into the prepared dish. Bake for 30 minutes or until the pudding does not shake when moved and is lightly brown on top.

Serves 1

Exchanges

2 1/2 Starch
1/2 Fat

Calories 217
 Calories from Fat . . . 54
Total Fat . . . . 6 g
 Saturated Fat . . . . 1 g
Cholesterol . . . . 1 mg
Sodium . . . . 157 mg
Carbohydrate . . . . 35 g
 Dietary Fiber . . . . 2 g
 Sugars . . . . 13 g
Protein . . . . 9 g

Cranberry and Orange Relish

Preparation Time: 10 minutes

This tangy mixture of fruits is pretty on your holiday table.

1/4 lb cranberries, washed and stems removed

1/4 cup unsweetened orange juice

1/4 cup water

1 stick cinnamon

2 tsp sugar

1 tsp ground cinnamon

1 large orange, peeled and cut into small pieces

1. Simmer the cranberries, orange juice, water, and cinnamon stick in a medium saucepan on low heat until the cranberries burst open. Remove from the heat and allow to cool.

2. When cool, add the sugar, cinnamon, and orange pieces. Refrigerate thoroughly before serving. Refrigerate any unused portion in a tightly sealed container.

Serves 2

Exchanges

1 1/2 Fruit

Calories 92
    Calories from Fat 2
Total Fat . . . . 0 g
    Saturated Fat . . . . 0 g
Cholesterol . . . . 0 mg
Sodium . . . . 1 mg
Carbohydrate . . . . 23 g
    Dietary Fiber . . . . 4 g
    Sugars . . . . 19 g
Protein . . . . 1 g

Cranberry Compote

Preparation Time: 10 minutes

Use prepared cranberry sauce to make this dish easier.

1/4 cup canned whole-berry cranberry sauce

1/2 ripe pear, peeled and cut into 1/2-inch pieces

2 dried apricot halves, chopped

1/2 cup unsweetened orange juice

2 dashes ground nutmeg

2 dashes ground cinnamon

1/2 tsp vanilla extract

1 Tbsp low-fat vanilla yogurt

1. Cook all ingredients except the yogurt in a small saucepan over low heat for about 15 minutes or until the pears are slightly soft.

2. Pour into a small serving dish. Garnish with yogurt and serve.

Serves 1

Exchanges

4 Carbohydrate

Calories 231
　Calories from Fat 7
Total Fat . . . . 1 g
　Saturated Fat . . . . . . 0 g
Cholesterol . . . . 1 mg
Sodium . . . . 27 mg
Carbohydrate . . . . . . 57 g
　Dietary Fiber . . . . . . 4 g
　Sugars . . . . 52 g
Protein . . . . 2 g

Dilled Peas

Preparation Time: 10 minutes

This is a refreshing change from standard garden salads to accompany a meal.

1 cup frozen tiny peas, thawed, rinsed, and drained

1/4 cup diced celery

1 Tbsp sweet red onion

1 Tbsp lite mayonnaise

1/4 tsp Worcestershire sauce

1 Tbsp low-fat sour cream

1/4 tsp dill

2 tsp sugar

Combine all the ingredients and refrigerate for 2 hours before serving.

Serves 2

Exchanges

1 Starch

Calories 94
  Calories from Fat 2
Total Fat . . . . 0 g
  Saturated Fat . . . . 0 g
Cholesterol . . . . 0 mg
Sodium . . . . 156 mg
Carbohydrate . . . . 19 g
  Dietary Fiber . . . . 5 g
  Sugars . . . . 10 g
Protein . . . . 5 g

Fast Spanish Rice

Preparation Time: 7 minutes

This is a great side dish for beef, pork, chicken, and even seafood!

1/2 cup instant cooked rice

2 Tbsp store-bought salsa

1/8 tsp cayenne pepper

2 tsp water

2 tsp chopped green chili

1 Tbsp chopped green onion

1. Combine all ingredients in a small bowl. Heat in a microwave-safe dish on high for 2 minutes or until hot, or heat in conventional saucepan over medium heat.

2. Serve immediately. Garnish with 2 tsp chopped black olives, if desired.

Serves 1

Exchanges

2 1/2 Starch

Calories 191
  Calories from Fat 1
Total Fat . . . . 0 g
  Saturated Fat . . . . 0 g
Cholesterol . . . . 0 mg
Sodium . . . . 86 mg
Carbohydrate . . . . 42 g
  Dietary Fiber . . . . 1 g
  Sugars . . . . 1 g
Protein . . . . 4 g

Gingery Baby Carrots

Preparation Time: 15 minutes

Try apple pie or pumpkin pie spice in this colorful side dish!

1/4 lb baby carrots, sliced julienne

1/4 cup unsweetened orange juice

1/4 tsp ground ginger

1/8 tsp nutmeg

1 Tbsp low-calorie margarine

1/2 tsp brown sugar

2 dashes salt

1 Tbsp chopped raisins

1. Place the carrots in a small saucepan and fill with water until the carrots are covered by 1 inch. Pour 2 Tbsp unsweetened orange juice into the saucepan and cook at medium heat until the carrots are slightly tender. Do not overcook.

2. Drain and place the carrots in a shallow serving dish and keep warm.

3. Combine the remaining orange juice, ginger, nutmeg, margarine, sugar, and salt in a small saucepan. Cook over low heat until the margarine is melted and the ingredients are blended.

4. Pour the sauce over the carrots. Garnish with the chopped raisins and serve.

Serves 2

Exchanges

1/2 Fruit
1 Vegetable
1/2 Fat

Calories 73
  Calories from Fat . . . 26
Total Fat . . . . 3 g
  Saturated Fat . . . . . . 1 g
Cholesterol . . . . 0 mg
Sodium . . . . 220 mg
Carbohydrate . . . . 12 g
  Dietary Fiber . . . . . . 2 g
  Sugars . . . . 8 g
Protein . . . . 1 g

Italian Drop Biscuits*

Preparation Time: 10 minutes

These taste great with soup, chili, or salad.

1 cup reduced-fat all-purpose baking mix

1/2 cup nonfat milk

1/4 cup shredded part-skim mozzarella cheese

1/2 tsp basil

1/4 tsp garlic powder

Dash cayenne pepper

1 tsp dried parsley

1. Preheat the oven to 450 degrees. Stir all the ingredients together in a small mixing bowl until a soft dough forms. Do not overstir. The dough should be sticky and heavy.

2. If the dough is too dry, stir in an additional Tbsp of nonfat milk. If it is too wet, add 1 Tbsp of reduced-fat all-purpose baking mix.

3. Drop the dough by spoonfuls onto an ungreased baking sheet.

4. Bake for 7–10 minutes or until the biscuits puff up and are light brown.

* This recipe is relatively high in sodium.

Serves 2

Exchanges

3 Starch
1/2 Fat

Calories	281
Calories from Fat	48
Total Fat	5 g
Saturated Fat	2 g
Cholesterol	9 mg
Sodium	819 mg
Carbohydrate	45 g
Dietary Fiber	1 g
Sugars	6 g
Protein	11 g

New Potatoes with Garlic

Preparation Time: 15 minutes

These chunky potatoes are good with steamed green beans and meat or seafood dishes.

5 new potatoes, unpeeled and quartered

1 tsp extra-virgin olive oil

2 cloves garlic, minced

1/2 tsp oregano

1/4 tsp onion powder

1. Preheat the oven to 325 degrees. Place the potatoes in a small bowl and drizzle olive oil over them. Toss gently to coat.

2. Add the garlic, stirring gently to combine. Sprinkle the oregano and onion powder over the potato mixture.

3. Place the potatoes in a nonstick baking pan and bake for 20–25 minutes or until the potatoes are soft.

Serves 1

Exchanges

3 Starch
1/2 Monounsaturated Fat

Calories	258
Calories from Fat	43
Total Fat	5 g
Saturated Fat	1 g
Cholesterol	0 mg
Sodium	16 mg
Carbohydrate	50 g
Dietary Fiber	5 g
Sugars	5 g
Protein	5 g

No-Fried Mexican Beans

Preparation Time: 15 minutes

You'll love this low-fat version of a classic Mexican side dish.

1/4 cup dried pinto beans, soaked for 8 hours, rinsed, and drained

1 tsp canola oil

2 Tbsp chopped onion

1 clove garlic, chopped

1/2 tsp ground cumin

Fresh ground pepper to taste

2 dashes cayenne pepper

1. Mash the beans using a potato masher and a sturdy bowl (or use a food processor). The beans should be broken up and mealy, but not completely pureed.

2. Heat the oil in a medium saucepan over medium heat. Saute the onions and garlic for 3–4 minutes until the onions are soft. Add the mashed beans, cumin, and peppers. Stir well.

3. Cook for 10–15 minutes, stirring occasionally, until some of the beans begin to brown and stick slightly. This browning action will help give the taste of authentic refried beans.

4. Cook until the desired consistency is achieved and serve.

Serves 1

Exchanges

2 Starch
1 Very Lean Meat
1/2 Monounsaturated Fat

Calories 219
  Calories from Fat . . . 48
Total Fat . . . . 5 g
  Saturated Fat . . . . 0 g
Cholesterol . . . . 0 mg
Sodium . . . . 6 mg
Carbohydrate . . . . . . 34 g
  Dietary Fiber . . . . . . 12 g
  Sugars . . . . 4 g
Protein . . . . 11 g

Presto Pesto Eggplant

Preparation Time: 10 minutes

This dish is good with rice, couscous, or pasta.

1 small eggplant, sliced in 1-inch circles

1 Tbsp prepared pesto sauce

1 small tomato, diced

Fresh ground black pepper to taste

1 Tbsp Parmesan cheese

2 Tbsp chopped fresh parsley

1. Preheat the oven to 350 degrees. Spray a baking sheet with nonstick cooking spray. Lay the eggplant slices on the baking sheet. Be sure the sides are not touching.

2. Coat the top of each slice with a thin layer of the pesto sauce.

3. Top each slice with a portion of the diced tomato. Sprinkle with the pepper, then the cheese.

4. Garnish with the parsley and bake for 15 minutes or until the eggplant is soft and the cheese is lightly golden.

Serves 2

Exchanges

1 Starch
(or 3 Vegetable)
1/2 Monounsaturated Fat

Calories 96
  Calories from Fat . . . 40
Total Fat . . . . 4 g
  Saturated Fat . . . . 1 g
Cholesterol . . . . 4 mg
Sodium . . . . 114 mg
Carbohydrate . . . . 13 g
  Dietary Fiber . . . . 5 g
  Sugars . . . . 8 g
Protein . . . . 4 g

Quick Pickled Vegetables

Preparation Time: 8 minutes

Ever have a handful of fresh vegetables left, and not know what to do with it? Use zucchini, yellow squash, peppers, carrots, cucumber, radish, cabbage, or a combination of these in this tangy side dish. Experiment with different vinegars—tarragon flavored, red wine, or cider—to create your own special taste.

1 cup thinly sliced zucchini

1/2 cup julienned or shaved carrots

1/4 cup water

1/4 cup white wine vinegar

2 tsp sugar

1. Put the zucchini and carrots in a small bowl.

2. Combine the water and vinegar in a small saucepan over medium-low heat. When the mixture is heated through, add the sugar and stir until the sugar is dissolved.

3. Quickly pour the hot vinegar and water mixture over the vegetables. Toss well and serve either hot or cold. For more intense flavor, let the vegetables sit for 15 minutes before serving.

Serves 1

Exchanges

2 Vegetable

Calories 52
  Calories from Fat 3
Total Fat . . . . 0 g
  Saturated Fat . . . . 0 g
Cholesterol . . . . 0 mg
Sodium . . . . 23 mg
Carbohydrate . . . . . . 12 g
  Dietary Fiber . . . . 3 g
  Sugars . . . . 9 g
Protein . . . . 2 g

Speedy Vegetables with Herbs

Preparation Time: 6 minutes

Canned carrots, beans, and mixed vegetables work best for this recipe. It is often less expensive to buy canned vegetables—here's a recipe that quickly seasons the vegetables to give them a fresh taste!

1/2 cup canned mixed
      vegetables, drained

1/2 tsp low-calorie margarine

1/2 tsp tarragon

1/8 tsp dill

  1 tsp lemon juice

1. Combine all ingredients in a small microwave-safe bowl. Microwave on high for 1 minute.

2. Stir, then microwave on high for 30–60 seconds, until the desired temperature is reached.

Serves 1

Exchanges

1/2 Starch

Calories 49
 Calories from Fat . . . 10
Total Fat . . . . 1 g
 Saturated Fat . . . . 0 g
Cholesterol . . . . 0 mg
Sodium . . . . 138 mg
Carbohydrate . . . . 8 g
 Dietary Fiber . . . . . . 2 g
 Sugars . . . . 3 g
Protein . . . . 2 g

Steamed Bay Rice

Preparation Time: 5 minutes

Seasoned rice tastes great as a side dish to seafood and other main dishes. Use any leftover rice as a bedding for a cold tuna salad the next day.

1/2 cup water

1/2 cup long-grain rice

  1 whole clove (or 1/8 tsp ground cloves)

  1 whole bay leaf

  1 Tbsp dried parsley

1/4 tsp paprika

1. Combine the water, rice, clove, and bay leaf in a small saucepan. Cover and bring to a boil over medium heat.

2. Reduce the heat and simmer until done. Remove the bay leaf and clove. Stir in the parsley and paprika to serve.

Serves 2

Exchanges

2 Starch

Calories 170
  Calories from Fat 3
Total Fat . . . . 0 g
  Saturated Fat . . . . 0 g
Cholesterol . . . . 0 mg
Sodium . . . . 3 mg
Carbohydrate . . . . 37 g
  Dietary Fiber . . . . 1 g
  Sugars . . . . 0 g
Protein . . . . 3 g

Luscious Desserts

Applesauce Cobbler

Preparation Time: 5 minutes

You can use chunky or smooth applesauce in this recipe

1 cup unsweetened applesauce

2 Tbsp crushed bran flakes cereal

1 Tbsp instant oatmeal

1/4 tsp cinnamon

Dash ground nutmeg

2 tsp sugar

1 tsp low-calorie margarine

1 tsp chopped nuts

1. Pour the applesauce in a small microwave-safe bowl.

2. Combine the remaining ingredients in a small zippered plastic bag. Use a rolling pin to help blend the mixture if desired. Sprinkle the mixture over the applesauce.

3. Cover and microwave on medium for 2 minutes. Let the cobbler stand for 2 minutes before serving.

Serves 1

Exchanges

3 Carbohydrate
1/2 Fat

Calories 202
  Calories from Fat . . . 32
Total Fat . . . . 4 g
  Saturated Fat . . . . . . 0 g
Cholesterol . . . . 0 mg
Sodium . . . . 87 mg
Carbohydrate . . . . . . 44 g
  Dietary Fiber . . . . 5 g
  Sugars . . . . 32 g
Protein . . . . 2 g

Baked Brandied Pears

Preparation Time: 15 minutes

Dried fruit can be used to top salads, fruits, and meat dishes, or to sweeten this baked dish!

1 large pear, peeled, halved, and cored

2 Tbsp chopped mixed dried fruit

1/2 tsp ground cinnamon

2 tsp brandy

1/4 cup unsweetened apple juice

2 Tbsp plain nonfat yogurt

1. Preheat the oven to 350 degrees. Spray a small baking dish with nonstick cooking spray.

2. Place the pear halves cut side up in the baking dish. Sprinkle each half with dried fruit, cinnamon, and brandy. Pour the apple juice into the bottom of the baking dish.

3. Bake for 20 minutes. Remove from the oven and let the pears cool for 5 minutes. When ready to serve, garnish with yogurt.

Serves 2

Exchanges

1 1/2 Fruit

Calories 97
  Calories from Fat 4
Total Fat . . . . 0 g
  Saturated Fat . . . . . . 0 g
Cholesterol . . . . 0 mg
Sodium . . . . 25 mg
Carbohydrate . . . . . . 22 g
  Dietary Fiber . . . . 3 g
  Sugars . . . . 17 g
Protein . . . . 1 g

Blackberry Turnovers with Glaze

Preparation Time: 15 minutes

Use prepared low-fat crescent roll dough as the pastry for these delicious turnovers! Be sure to freeze the leftovers for another day.

1   8-oz can low-fat crescent roll dough

1/4   cup fruit-sweetened blackberry jam

3   Tbsp nonfat milk

1/4   cup powdered sugar

1/4   tsp fresh lemon juice

1/4   tsp grated lemon peel

1. Preheat the oven as directed on the crescent roll package. Separate the dough into 8 triangles, as per package directions.

2. Take one triangle and place on a prepared baking sheet. Place 1 1/2 tsp jam in the center of the triangle. To create the turnover, fold the long ends of the triangle over on each other, making a smaller triangle. Seal the seams with your fingers or a fork. Repeat with each triangle of dough.

3. Put 1 Tbsp of the nonfat milk in a small cup and brush each turnover with the milk. Bake as directed per package instructions. The turnovers should be lightly brown. Remove them from the oven promptly and place the turnovers onto a clean plate to cool slightly.

4. Combine the remaining ingredients in a small bowl and mix until smooth. Spoon glaze over the slightly cooled turnovers and serve immediately.

Serves 4

Exchanges

2 1/2 Carbohydrate
1 1/2 Fat

Calories 256
  Calories from Fat . . 81
Total Fat . . . . 9 g
  Saturated Fat . . . . . . 2 g
Cholesterol . . . . 0 mg
Sodium . . . . 472 mg
Carbohydrate . . . . . . 38 g
  Dietary Fiber . . . . . . 1 g
  Sugars . . . . 16 g
Protein . . . . 4 g

Chocolate Kisses

Preparation Time: 5 minutes

These are a low-sugar treat! Use butterscotch or other pudding flavors for variety.

1   1.4-oz pkg fat-free, sugar-free, instant chocolate pudding

1   cup nonfat milk

1. Whisk together the pudding mix and the milk in a small bowl until the batter is pasty. Cover a small, flat, metal (not glass) tray or plate with waxed paper.

2. With a large spoon or a tablespoon measure, drop the batter on the tray to form 12 large drop shapes resembling the commercial candy. (A small cake-decorating bag with a large round tip makes the job a breeze!)

3. Freeze until hard. Store on a flat tray in the refrigerator or layered between waxed paper in a small covered container.

Serves 4

Exchanges

1/2 Carbohydrate

Calories 57
  Calories from Fat   . . . 1
Total Fat . . . . 0 g
  Saturated Fat   . . . . . . 0 g
Cholesterol . . . . 1 mg
Sodium . . . . 142 mg
Carbohydrate . . . . . . 11 g
  Dietary Fiber . . . . 1 g
  Sugars . . . . 3 g
Protein . . . . 3 g

Cinnamon Apple Rings

Preparation Time: 12 minutes

This dessert will warm you up on a cold fall day!

2 Tbsp all-purpose flour

2 dashes ground cinnamon

2 tsp sugar

1 large Granny Smith apple, unpeeled, cored, and sliced in 1/2-inch rings

2 tsp low-calorie margarine

1 Tbsp chopped golden raisins

1. Combine the flour, cinnamon, and sugar in a small plastic zippered bag. Shake the bag to mix well. Place one apple ring into the bag and shake to coat the apple ring with the flour mixture. Remove the apple ring and place on a plate. Repeat with all the apple rings.

2. Melt the margarine in a small skillet over medium-high heat. Add the apple rings, cooking for about 5 minutes per side until light brown and slightly soft. Drain the apples on paper towels, place them on a serving plate, and sprinkle them with the raisins. Serve hot.

Serves 1

Exchanges

4 Carbohydrate
1/2 Fat

Calories 276
  Calories from Fat . . 43
Total Fat . . . . 5 g
  Saturated Fat . . . . . . 1 g
Cholesterol . . . . 0 mg
Sodium . . . . 62 mg
Carbohydrate . . . . . . 60 g
  Dietary Fiber . . . . 7 g
  Sugars . . . . 41 g
Protein . . . . 2 g

Fruited Frozen Yogurt

Preparation Time: 2 minutes

The key to this dessert is its eye appeal! Presenting an old favorite differently can add variety to your meal plan.

1/8 whole cantaloupe

1/2 cup frozen yogurt (citrus, coconut, or other fruit flavors are good)

10 grapes, sliced

1. Using a melon baller, scoop the cantaloupe flesh into balls and place on a serving dish.

2. Continue using the melon baller to scoop the frozen yogurt into balls and add them to the cantaloupe. Top with sliced grapes and serve.

Serves 1

Exchanges

2 Carbohydrate
1/2 Saturated Fat

Calories 159
　Calories from Fat . . 27
Total Fat . . . . 3 g
　Saturated Fat . . . . . . 2 g
Cholesterol . . . . 10 mg
Sodium . . . . 37 mg
Carbohydrate . . . . . . 32 g
　Dietary Fiber . . . . . . 1 g
　Sugars . . . . 26 g
Protein . . . . 4 g

Hawaiian Isle Sorbet

Preparation Time: 2 minutes

Try this refreshing treat on a hot summer day.

2 pineapple slices, canned in their own juice

1/2 cup raspberry sorbet

2 Tbsp nonfat whipped topping

1. Place one slice of pineapple on a dessert plate. Using a melon baller, scoop out 4 or 5 small balls of sorbet.

2. Top with a twisted pineapple slice. Garnish with whipped topping and serve at once.

Serves 1

Exchanges

3 1/2 Carbohydrate

Calories 204
    Calories from Fat . . . 1
Total Fat . . . . 0 g
    Saturated Fat . . . . . . 0 g
Cholesterol . . . . 0 mg
Sodium . . . . 11 mg
Carbohydrate . . . . . . 50 g
    Dietary Fiber . . . . 1 g
    Sugars . . . . 46 g
Protein . . . . 1 g

Heavenly Parfait

Preparation Time: 5 minutes

The secret to this dessert is having angel food cake crumbs! Tear a fresh cake into pieces the size of nickels and dimes. Freeze in 1-cup portions in plastic zippered bags. Thaw to use as a topping or bedding for fresh fruit, fruit compotes, yogurt, sherbets, frozen yogurt, or ice cream. For extra flavor, lightly toast the crumbs.

1 cup prepared fat-free, sugar-free pudding (any flavor)

1 cup angel food cake crumbs (thaw if frozen)

1 Tbsp nondairy whipped topping

1. In a large wine or parfait glass, spoon 1/2 cup of the prepared pudding into the bottom of the glass. Add half of the cake crumbs.

2. Top with the remaining pudding and the rest of the crumbs. Add nondairy whipped topping or fresh fruit and serve.

Serves 1
Exchanges
3 1/2 Carbohydrate

Calories	292
Calories from Fat	11
Total Fat	1 g
Saturated Fat	1 g
Cholesterol	4 mg
Sodium	431 mg
Carbohydrate	56 g
Dietary Fiber	3 g
Sugars	28 g
Protein	14 g

Incredible Crepes

Preparation Time: 30 minutes

Making crepes in a regular skillet is easy. Here's how!

1/2 cup nonfat milk

1/3 cup all-purpose flour

1 egg

4 1/2 tsp sugar

Dash ground nutmeg

1 small orange, peeled and seeds removed

1 tsp low-calorie margarine

1/4 cup unsweetened orange juice

1 tsp cornstarch

1/2 tsp vanilla

1 Tbsp low-fat sour cream

1. Whisk together the milk, flour, egg, sugar, and nutmeg in a small bowl until frothy and refrigerate for at least 1 hour. Meanwhile, cut away the rind and membranes of the orange so that only the fruit flesh remains. Chop the orange flesh into small pieces.

2. When the batter is ready, melt the margarine in a small skillet over medium heat, rolling the skillet to completely coat it with the margarine. Using a small ladle, pour approximately 2 Tbsp of batter into the heated skillet, again rolling the skillet to quickly coat the bottom.

3. Using a plastic flexible spatula, turn the crepe when the edges begin to brown slightly. Cook

(continued)

Serves 2

Exchanges

3 Carbohydrate
1 Very Lean Meat
1/2 Fat

Calories 238
  Calories from Fat . . 40
Total Fat . . . . 4 g
  Saturated Fat . . . . . . 1 g
Cholesterol . . . . 110 mg
Sodium . . . . 82 mg
Carbohydrate . . . . . 41 g
  Dietary Fiber . . . . 2 g
  Sugars . . . . 22 g
Protein . . . . 8 g

Incredible Crepes

(*continued*)

the other side until it is also light brown. Remove the crepe from the pan quickly, fold it into quarters, and place it on a cool plate. Repeat until all the batter is used.

4. Mix together 1 Tbsp of the orange juice with the cornstarch until smooth. Return the small skillet to the heat and add the remaining orange juice and orange pieces, cooking until bubbly. Quickly add the cornstarch mixture and stir constantly with a wooden spoon.

5. When the mixture begins to thicken slightly, add the vanilla and stir well. Gently add the folded crepes back into the skillet, and swirl the skillet to coat the crepes with the sauce. The sauce should be slightly thickened, just enough to coat a spoon. (Add a mixture of another 1/2 tsp cornstarch and 1 tsp water if needed to further thicken the sauce.)

6. When all the crepes are thoroughly heated, divide the contents of the skillet onto two serving plates, top each with sour cream, and serve. If you like, before removing the crepes from the heat, turn the heat to high, add 2 Tbsp Gran Marnier or brandy, and flame before serving.

Jammin' Cookies

Preparation Time: 20 minutes

Use prepared refrigerator cookie dough to make this easy treat.

- 4 1/4-inch-thick slices sugar cookie dough
- 1 Tbsp fruit-sweetened strawberry or cherry jam
- 1 egg yolk
- 2–3 drops food coloring

1. Preheat the oven as directed to bake the cookies. Roll the cookie dough pieces out to approximately 4 inches in diameter. You may need to dust the rolling pin with flour to prevent it from sticking.

2. Place approximately 1 1/2 tsp jam in the center of each of 2 cookies. Top the jam-filled cookies with the remaining cookies, aligning the edges. Place the cookies on a prepared baking sheet as directed on the cookie dough package.

3. Beat the egg yolk in a small bowl until it is light and frothy. Add the food coloring and stir to mix. Dip a fork into the colored egg yolk and press it down on the edges of each cookie about 1/4 inch all around to seal. Bake as directed on the package.

4. You can use a clean cotton swab or a tiny paint brush to add additional designs on the cookies! Dip the brush into the egg yolk mixture and paint them just before baking.

Serves 2

Exchanges

3 Carbohydrate
2 1/2 Monounsaturated Fat

Calories	334
Calories from Fat	142
Total Fat	16 g
Saturated Fat	4 g
Cholesterol	125 mg
Sodium	273 mg
Carbohydrate	45 g
Dietary Fiber	1 g
Sugars	25 g
Protein	4 g

Peach Melba Cobbler

Preparation Time: 25 minutes

Any type of frozen, unsweetened fruit can be substituted for the peaches and raspberries in this recipe.

1/2 cup canned, sliced peaches in juice, drained

1/2 cup frozen raspberries

1/2 tsp cornstarch

1/2 tsp water

 4 tsp sugar

1/3 cup reduced-fat, all-purpose baking mix

 7 tsp nonfat milk

1. Preheat the oven to 400 degrees. Combine the peaches and raspberries in a small, ungreased, microwave- and oven-safe casserole dish. Microwave on high for 4 minutes, or until heated through.

2. Mix together the cornstarch and water until smooth. Add this mixture to the fruit and stir well. Return the fruit mixture to the microwave and heat on high for 30 seconds or until the juice is slightly thickened. Sprinkle 2 tsp sugar on top and set aside.

3. Combine the baking mix, remaining sugar, and milk. Stir to moisten, but do not overmix. Form a soft dough ball with your hands and turn

(continued)

Serves 2

Exchanges

2 1/2 Carbohydrate

Calories 158
  Calories from Fat . . 13
Total Fat . . . . 1 g
  Saturated Fat . . . . . . 0 g
Cholesterol . . . . 1 mg
Sodium . . . . 241 mg
Carbohydrate . . . . . . 34 g
  Dietary Fiber . . . . 3 g
  Sugars . . . . 18 g
Protein . . . . 3 g

Peach Melba Cobbler

(continued)

the dough out on a board sprinkled lightly with flour or extra baking mix.

4. Roll out the dough to the approximate size of the casserole dish to serve as a loose cover for the fruit mixture. Place the dough on top of the hot fruit.

5. Heat the cobbler in a conventional oven for 10 minutes, or until the dough is lightly browned and puffed and the fruit is bubbly. Serve immediately.

Speedy Fruit Compote

Preparation Time: 10 minutes

This compote can be used as a dessert or side dish, or as a topping for pancakes, waffles, yogurt, or ice cream.

1/4 pear, peeled, cored, and chopped

1/4 orange, peeled and chopped

1/4 apple, peeled, cored, and chopped

1 Tbsp dehydrated cranberries

1 Tbsp unsweetened orange juice

1. Combine all ingredients in a small microwave-safe bowl. (You may substitute raisins, dried apricots, or dried pineapples for the cranberries.) Cover with plastic wrap and microwave on high for 3 minutes.

2. For extra flavor, sprinkle with cinnamon or 2 Tbsp crushed, whole-grain cereal.

Serves 1

Exchanges

2 Fruit

Calories 121
    Calories from Fat . . . 6
Total Fat . . . . 1 g
    Saturated Fat . . . . . . 0 g
Cholesterol . . . . 0 mg
Sodium . . . . 1 mg
Carbohydrate . . . . . . 31 g
    Dietary Fiber . . . . 7 g
    Sugars . . . . 24 g
Protein . . . . 1 g

Spicy Fruit with Yogurt

Preparation Time: 15 minutes

Great for a cold night!

1/4 cup water

1/4 cup unsweetened orange juice

1/2 pear, peeled, cored, and cut into 1/2-inch pieces

4 dried apricot halves, cut into 4–6 pieces each

1 small orange, peeled, seeds removed, and cut into 1/2-inch pieces

1/2 grapefruit, peeled, seeds removed, and cut into 1/2-inch pieces

1/4 lb fresh cranberries, stems removed and washed

4 tsp sugar

2 dashes nutmeg

1/4 tsp cinnamon

1/2 tsp vanilla extract

2 oz low-fat unsweetened vanilla yogurt

Dash cinnamon

1. Combine the water and orange juice in a medium saucepan and bring to a boil. Reduce the heat to low and add the pears and apricots. Cook for 5 minutes or until softened. Add the orange and grapefruit and simmer for 5 minutes.

2. Turn the heat up to medium, add the cranberries and sugar, and cook until the cranberries burst open, stirring often.

3. Add the nutmeg, cinnamon, and vanilla and remove from heat. Allow the mixture to cool slightly. Serve the compote warm in a small dish with a dollop of yogurt and a sprinkle of cinnamon.

Serves 2
Exchanges
3 1/2 Carbohydrate

Calories 205
  Calories from Fat . . . 9
Total Fat . . . . 1 g
  Saturated Fat . . . . . . 0 g
Cholesterol . . . . 3 mg
Sodium . . . . 19 mg
Carbohydrate . . . . . . 50 g
  Dietary Fiber . . . . 7 g
  Sugars . . . . 41 g
Protein . . . . 3 g

Strawberry Ice Cream Sandwich

Preparation Time: 3 minutes

Relive your childhood with this appealing snack!

1 reduced fat, artificially sweetened ice cream sandwich, halved horizontally

2 Tbsp fruit-sweetened strawberry jam

1/4 cup fat-free whipped topping

1/4 cup sliced fresh strawberries

1. Place half of the ice cream sandwich on a serving plate. Spread 2 Tbsp of the strawberry jam on top. Place the other sandwich half on top of the jam.

2. Cover the top and sides evenly with the whipped topping. Garnish with the sliced strawberries and serve immediately.

Serves 1

Exchanges

3 Carbohydrate
1/2 Saturated Fat

Calories 246
  Calories from Fat . . 37
Total Fat . . . . 4 g
  Saturated Fat . . . . . . 2 g
Cholesterol . . . . 10 mg
Sodium . . . . 139 mg
Carbohydrate . . . . . 47 g
  Dietary Fiber . . . . . . 2 g
  Sugars . . . . 13 g
Protein . . . . 4 g

Pudding Tarts

Preparation Time: 25 minutes

This is a nice dessert to serve when you have a friend over for dinner.

3 Tbsp plus 1 tsp fat-free, artificially sweetened instant pudding mix, any flavor

6 Tbsp nonfat milk

1/2 cup frozen, unsweetened, pitted cherries

1/2 tsp cornstarch

1/2 tsp cold water

2 graham cracker tart shells (available in the grocery store baking aisle)

1. Whisk together the pudding mix and nonfat milk until smooth and thickened.

2. In a small microwave-safe bowl, microwave the frozen cherries on high for 1 1/2 minutes until the cherries are soft and the juice is released. Do not drain!

3. Mix the cornstarch and water together until smooth. Add the cornstarch mixture to the cherries, stir, and return to the microwave. Microwave on high for 30 seconds, or until the cherry mixture is thick.

4. Place the graham cracker tart shells on a small plate. Carefully spoon half of the pudding mixture into each shell and top with the cherry mixture. Refrigerate for 1 hour or until ready to serve.

Serves 2

Exchanges

2 Carbohydrate
1 Fat

Calories 211
  Calories from Fat . . 54
Total Fat . . . . 6 g
  Saturated Fat . . . . . . 1 g
Cholesterol . . . . 1 mg
Sodium . . . . 320 mg
Carbohydrate . . . . . . 33 g
  Dietary Fiber . . . . 2 g
  Sugars . . . . 11 g
Protein . . . . 4 g

Wisconsin Apple Bread

Preparation Time: 15 minutes

This is delicious bread to eat for brunch, lunch, or as a snack.

1 cup all-purpose flour

2 1/2 Tbsp sugar

3/4 tsp baking powder

1/4 tsp salt

1/4 tsp allspice

1/4 cup nonfat milk

1 egg

1 Tbsp canola oil

1 tsp vanilla

1/4 cup shredded, low-fat sharp cheddar cheese

1/2 cup chopped tart apples

1. Preheat the oven to 350 degrees. Spray a mini loaf pan (5 1/2 × 3 1/4 inches) with nonstick cooking spray.

2. Combine the flour, sugar, baking powder, salt, and allspice in a small bowl. In a separate bowl, whisk together the milk, egg, oil, and vanilla until frothy.

3. Add the liquid mixture to the dry mixture and stir until just blended. Add the cheese and chopped apples and stir gently.

4. Spoon the mixture into the prepared loaf pan and bake for 35–40 minutes, or until a toothpick comes out clean when inserted into the center of the loaf. Allow the apple bread to cool completely. Cut into 6 slices and serve.

Serves 3

Exchanges

3 Starch
1 Monounsaturated Fat

Calories 298
  Calories from Fat   . . 73
Total Fat . . . . 8 g
  Saturated Fat . . . . . . 2 g
Cholesterol . . . . 76 mg
Sodium . . . . 370 mg
Carbohydrate . . . . . . 45 g
  Dietary Fiber . . . . 1 g
  Sugars . . . . 13 g
Protein . . . . 10 g

Index

About the American Diabetes Association

The American Diabetes Association is the nation's leading voluntary health organization supporting diabetes research, information, and advocacy. Its mission is to prevent and cure diabetes and to improve the lives of all people affected by diabetes. The American Diabetes Association is the leading publisher of comprehensive diabetes information. Its huge library of practical and authoritative books for people with diabetes covers every aspect of self-care—cooking and nutrition, fitness, weight control, medications, complications, emotional issues, and general self-care.

To order American Diabetes Association books: Call 1-800-232-6733. http://store.diabetes.org [Note: there is no need to use **www** when typing this particular Web address]

To join the American Diabetes Association: Call 1-800-806-7801. www.diabetes.org/membership

For more information about diabetes or ADA programs and services: Call 1-800-342-2383. E-mail: Customerservice@diabetes.org

To locate an ADA/NCQA Recognized Provider of quality diabetes care in your area: Call 1-703-549-1500 ext. 2202. www.diabetes.org/recognition/Physicians/ListAll.asp

To find an ADA Recognized Education Program in your area: Call 1-888-232-0822. www.diabetes.org/recognition/education.asp

To join the fight to increase funding for diabetes research, end discrimination, and improve insurance coverage: Call 1-800-342-2383. www.diabetes.org/advocacy

To find out how you can get involved with the programs in your community: Call 1-800-342-2383. See below for program Web addresses.

- *American Diabetes Month:* Educational activities aimed at those diagnosed with diabetes—month of November. www.diabetes.org/ADM

- *American Diabetes Alert:* Annual public awareness campaign to find the undiagnosed—held the fourth Tuesday in March. www.diabetes.org/alert

- *The Diabetes Assistance & Resources Program (DAR):* diabetes awareness program targeted to the Latino community. www.diabetes.org/DAR

- *African American Program:* diabetes awareness program targeted to the African American community. www.diabetes.org/africanamerican\

- *Awakening the Spirit: Pathways to Diabetes Prevention & Control:* diabetes awareness program targeted to the Native American community. www.diabetes.org/awakening

To find out about an important research project regarding type 2 diabetes: www.diabetes.org/ada/research.asp

To obtain information on making a planned gift or charitable bequest: Call 1-888-700-7029. www.diabetes.org/ada/plan.asp

To make a donation or memorial contribution: Call 1-800-342-2383. www.diabetes.org/ada/cont.asp